DEPARTMENT OF THE NAVY
HEADQUARTERS UNITED STATES MARINE CORPS
3000 MARINE CORPS PENTAGON
WASHINGTON, D.C. 20350-3000

I0425943

COMMAND AND CONTROL (C2) TRAINING AND READINESS (T&R) MANUAL

DEPARTMENT OF THE NAVY
HEADQUARTERS UNITED STATES MARINE CORPS
3000 MARINE CORPS PENTAGON
WASHINGTON, D.C. 20350-3000

NAVMC 3500.54B
C 469
23 Aug 2011

NAVMC 3500.54B W/CH 1

From: Commandant of the Marine Corps
To: Distribution List

Subj: COMMAND AND CONTROL (C2) TRAINING AND READINESS (T&R) MANUAL

Ref: (a) MCO P3500.72A
      (b) MCO 1553.3A
      (c) MCO 3400.3F
      (d) MCO 3500.27B W/Erratum
      (e) MCRP 3-0A
      (f) MCRP 3-0B
      (g) MCO 1553.2B

1. Purpose. Per references (a) through (g), this T&R Manual establishes
training standards, regulations, and practices regarding the C2 training of
Marines who require skills to effectively prepare other Marines for combat in
formal school environments.

2. Cancellation. NAVMC 3500.54A

3. Scope

    a. Formal school and training detachment commanders will use references
(a) and (b) to ensure program of instruction meet skill-training requirements
established in this manual and provide career-progression training in the
events designated for initial training in the formal school environment.

    b. Per reference (b), commanders will conduct an internal assessment of
the unit's ability to execute its mission and develop long-, mid-, and short-
range training plans to sustain proficiency and correct deficiencies.
Training plans will incorporate these events to standardize training and
provide objective assessment of progress toward attaining combat readiness.
Commanders will keep records at the unit and individual levels to record
training achievements, identify training gaps and document objective
assessments of readiness associated with training Marines. Commanders will
use reference (d) to integrate Operational Risk Management (ORM). References
(e) and (f) provide amplifying information for effective planning and
management of training within the unit.

4. Information. Commanding General (CG), Training and Education Command
(TECOM) will update this T&R Manual as necessary to provide current and
relevant training standards to commanders. All questions pertaining to the
Marine Corps Ground T&R Program and Unit Training Management should be
directed to: CG, TECOM (Ground Training Division C 469), 1019 Elliot Road,
Quantico, VA 22134.

5. <u>Command</u>. This Manual is applicable to the Marine Corps Total Force.

6. <u>Certification</u>. Reviewed and approved this date.

R. C. FOX
By direction

DISTRIBUTION: PCN 10031977500

   Copy to: 7000260 (2)
            8145001 (1)

DEPARTMENT OF THE NAVY
HEADQUARTERS UNITED STATES MARINE CORPS
3000 MARINE CORPS PENTAGON
WASHINGTON, D.C. 20350-3000

NAVMC 3500.54B Ch 1
C 469
1 5 DEC 2011

NAVMC 3500.54B Ch 1

From: Commandant of the Marine Corps
To: Distribution List

Subj: COMMAND AND CONTROL (C2) TRAINING AND READINESS (T&R) MANUAL

Encl: (1) New page inserts to NAVMC 3500.54B

1. Purpose. To transmit page inserts to the Manual.

2. Scope. Remove pages 4-5 and replace with corresponding pages in the enclosure. Insert new pages 4-37 through 4-41 at the end of chapter 4 of the basic Manual.

3. Information. This change is out of the normal T&R review cycle. After further discussion between the C2 Advocate, C2 Training and Education Center of Excellence (TECOE) and Training and Education Command (TECOM), it was determined the previously omitted Attack the Network individual events should be included in Change 1 to the C2 T&R Manual.

4. Filing Instructions. This change transmittal will be filed immediately following the signature page of the Manual.

R. C. FOX
By direction

DISTRIBUTION: PCN 10033194600

Copy to: 7000260 (2)
          8145001 (1)

DISTRIBUTION STATEMENT A: Approved for public release; distribution is unlimited.

LOCATOR SHEET

Subj: COMMAND AND CONTROL (C2) TRAINING AND READINESS (T&R) MANUAL

Location: _____

(Indicate location(s) of copy(ies) of this Manual.)

RECORD OF CHANGES

Log completed change action as indicated

Change Number	Date of Change	Date Entered	Signature of Person Incorporated Change

C2 T&R MANUAL

TABLE OF CONTENTS

CHAPTER 1

OVERVIEW

CHAPTER 1

OVERVIEW

1000. INTRODUCTION

1. The T&R Program is the Corps' primary tool for planning, conducting and evaluating training and assessing training readiness. Core MET workshops, hosted by DC CD&I and supported by Service Advocates, MARFORCOM, and unit commanders or their representatives, develop standardized core Mission Essential Tasks (METs) for all Marine Corps units (CE, Ground, Aviation, Logistics, and Installations). The METs used to build these METLS are selected from the Marine Corps Task List (MCTL). T&R Manuals are built around these METLs and all events contained in T&R Manuals relate directly to this METL. This comprehensive T&R Program will help to ensure the Marine Corps continues to improve its combat readiness by training more efficiently and effectively. Ultimately, this will enhance the Marine Corps' ability to accomplish real-world missions.

2. The T&R Manual contains the individual and collective training requirements to prepare units to accomplish their combat mission. The T&R Manual is not intended to be an encyclopedia that contains every minute detail of how to accomplish training. Instead, it identifies the minimum standards that Marines must be able to perform in combat. The T&R Manual is a fundamental tool for commanders to build and maintain unit combat readiness. Using this tool, leaders can construct and execute an effective training plan that supports the unit's METL. More detailed information on the Marine Corps Ground T&R Program is found in reference (a).

1001. UNIT TRAINING

1. The training of Marines to perform as an integrated unit in combat lies at the heart of the T&R program. Unit and individual readiness are directly related. Individual training and the mastery of individual core skills serve as the building blocks for unit combat readiness. A Marine's ability to perform critical skills required in combat is essential. However, it is not necessary to have all individuals within a unit fully trained in order for that organization to accomplish its assigned tasks. Manpower shortfalls, temporary assignments, leave, or other factors outside the commander's control, often affect the ability to conduct individual training. During these periods, unit readiness is enhanced if emphasis is placed on the individual training of Marines on-hand. Subsequently, these Marines will be mission ready and capable of executing as part of a team when the full complement of personnel is available.

2. Commanders will ensure that all tactical training is focused on their combat mission. The T&R Manual is a tool to help develop the unit's training plan. In most cases, unit training should focus on achieving unit proficiency in core METs. However, commanders may adjust their training focus to support METs required for assigned missions (e.g., pre-deployment

PTP requirements), or METs associated with a major OPLAN/CONPLAN or named operation as designated by their higher commander. Designated units report their readiness to perform METs in the Defense Readiness Reporting System - Marine Corps (DRRS-MC). Tactical training will support the METL in use by the commander and be tailored to meet T&R standards. Commanders at all levels are responsible for effective combat training. The conduct of training in a professional manner consistent with Marine Corps standards cannot be over emphasized.

3. Commanders will provide personnel the opportunity to attend formal and operational level courses of instruction as required by this Manual. Attendance at all formal courses must enhance the warfighting capabilities of the unit as determined by the unit commander.

1002. UNIT TRAINING MANAGEMENT

1. Unit Training Management (UTM) is the application of the Systems Approach to Training (SAT) and the Marine Corps Training Principles. This is accomplished in a manner that maximizes training results and focuses the training priorities of the unit in preparation for the conduct of its wartime mission.

2. UTM techniques, described in references (b) and (e), provide commanders with the requisite tools and techniques to analyze, design, develop, implement, and evaluate the training of their unit. The Marine Corps Training Principles, explained in reference (b), provide sound and proven direction and are flexible enough to accommodate the demands of local conditions. These principles are not inclusive, nor do they guarantee success. They are guides that commanders can use to manage unit-training programs. The Marine Corps training principles are:

- Train as you fight
- Make commanders responsible for training
- Use standards-based training
- Use performance-oriented training
- Use mission-oriented training
- Train the MAGTF to fight as a combined arms team
- Train to sustain proficiency
- Train to challenge

3. To maintain an efficient and effective training program, leaders at every level must understand and implement UTM. Guidance for UTM and the process for establishing effective programs are contained in references (a) through (g).

1003. SUSTAINMENT AND EVALUATION OF TRAINING

1. The evaluation of training is necessary to properly prepare Marines for combat. Evaluations are either formal or informal, and performed by members of the unit (internal evaluation) or from an external command (external evaluation).

2. Marines are expected to maintain proficiency in the training events for their MOS at the appropriate grade or billet to which assigned. Leaders are responsible for recording the training achievements of their Marines. Whether it involves individual or collective training events, they must ensure proficiency is sustained by requiring retraining of each event at or before expiration of the designated sustainment interval. Performance of the training event, however, is not sufficient to ensure combat readiness. Leaders at all levels must evaluate the performance of their Marines and the unit as they complete training events, and only record successful accomplishment of training based upon the evaluation. The goal of evaluation is to ensure that correct methods are employed to achieve the desired standard, or the Marines understand how they need to improve in order to attain the standard. Leaders must determine whether credit for completing a training event is recorded if the standard was not achieved. While successful accomplishment is desired, debriefing of errors can result in successful learning that will allow ethical recording of training event completion. Evaluation is a continuous process that is integral to training management and is conducted by leaders at every level and during all phases of planning and the conduct of training. To ensure training is efficient and effective, evaluation is an integral part of the training plan. Ultimately, leaders remain responsible for determining if the training was effective.

3. The purpose of formal and informal evaluation is to provide commanders with a process to determine a unit's/Marine's proficiency in the tasks that must be performed in combat. Informal evaluations are conducted during every training evolution. Formal evaluations are often scenario-based, focused on the unit's METs, based on collective training standards, and usually conducted during higher-level collective events. References (a) and (f) provide further guidance on the conduct of informal and formal evaluations using the Marine Corps Ground T&R Program.

1004. ORGANIZATION

1. T&R Manuals are organized in one of two methods: unit-based or community-based. Unit-based T&R Manuals are written to support a type of unit (Infantry, Artillery, Tanks, etc.) and contain both collective and individual training standards. Community-based are written to support an Occupational Field, a group of related Military Occupational Specialties (MOSs), or billets within an organization (EOD, NBC, Intel, etc.), and usually only contain individual training standards. T&R Manuals are comprised of chapters that contain unit METs, collective training standards (CTS), and individual training standards (ITS) for each MOS, billet, etc.

2. The C2 T&R Manual is a unit-based manual comprised of 4 chapters. Chapter 2 lists the Core Capability METs and their related Battalion and Company-level events. Chapter 3 contains collective events. Chapter 4 contains individual events.

1005. T&R EVENT CODING

1. T&R events are coded for ease of reference. Each event has up-to a 4-4-4-digit identifier. The first up-to four digits are referred to as a "community" and represent the unit type or occupation (TANK, TOW, 1802,

etc.). The second up-to four digits represent the functional or duty area
(TAC, CMDC, GNRY, etc.). The last four digits represent the level and
sequence of the event.

2. The T&R levels are illustrated in Figure 1. An example of the T&R coding
used in this Manual is shown in Figure 2.

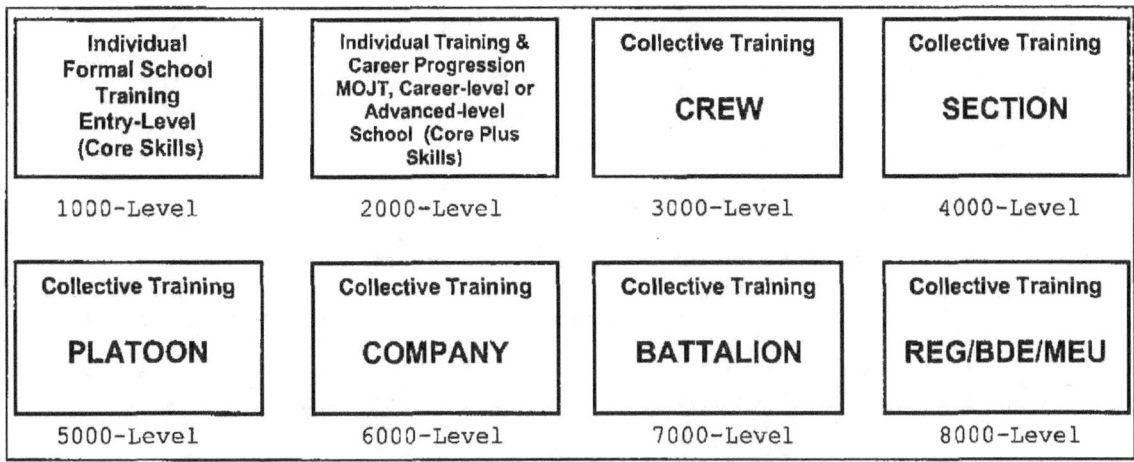

Figure 1: T&R Event Levels

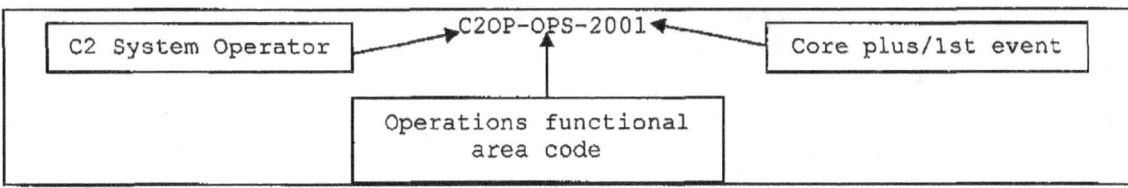

Figure 2: T&R Event Coding

1006. COMBAT READINESS PERCENTAGE

1. The Marine Corps Ground T&R Program includes processes to assess
readiness of units and individual Marines. Every unit in the Marine Corps
maintains a basic level of readiness based on the training and experience of
the Marines in the unit. Even units that never trained together are capable
of accomplishing some portion of their missions. Combat readiness assessment
does not associate a quantitative value for this baseline of readiness, but
uses a "Combat Readiness Percentage", as a method to provide a concise
descriptor of the recent training accomplishments of units and Marines.

2. Combat Readiness Percentage (CRP) is the percentage of required training
events that a unit or Marine accomplishes within specified sustainment
intervals.

3. In unit-based T&R Manuals, unit combat readiness is assessed as a
percentage of the successfully completed and current (within sustainment
interval) key training events called "Evaluation-Coded" (E-Coded) Events. E-
Coded Events and unit CRP calculation are described in follow-on paragraphs.

CRP achieved through the completion of E-Coded Events is directly relevant to readiness assessment in DRRS.

4.   Individual combat readiness, in both unit-based and community-based T&R Manuals, is assessed as the percentage of required individual events in which a Marine is current. This translates as the percentage of training events for his/her MOS and grade (or billet) that the Marine successfully completes within the directed sustainment interval. Individual skills are developed through a combination of 1000-level training (entry-level formal school courses), individual on-the-job training in 2000-level events, and follow-on formal school training. Skill proficiency is maintained by retraining in each event per the specified sustainment interval.

1007.   EVALUATION-CODED (E-CODED) EVENTS

1.   Unit-type T&R Manuals can contain numerous unit events, some for the whole unit and others for integral parts that serve as building blocks for training. To simplify training management and readiness assessment, only collective events that are critical components of a mission essential task (MET), or key indicators of a unit's readiness, are used to generate CRP for a MET. These critical or key events are designated in the T&R Manual as Evaluation-Coded (E-Coded) events. Formal evaluation of unit performance in these events is recommended because of their value in assessing combat readiness. Only E-Coded events are used to calculate CRP for each MET.

2.   The use of a METL-based training program allows the commander discretion in training. This makes the T&R Manual a training tool rather than a prescriptive checklist.

1008.   CRP CALCULATION

1.   Collective training begins at the 3000 level (team, crew or equivalent). Unit training plans are designed to accomplish the events that support the unit METL while simultaneously sustaining proficiency in individual core skills. Using the battalion-based (unit) model, the battalion (7000-level) has collective events that directly support a MET on the METL. These collective events are E-Coded and the only events that contribute to unit CRP. This is done to assist commanders in prioritizing the training toward the METL, taking into account resource, time, and personnel constraints.

2.   Unit CRP increases after the completion of E-Coded events. The number of E-Coded events for the MET determines the value of each E-Coded event. For example, if there are 4 E-Coded events for a MET, each is worth 25% of MET CRP. MET CRP is calculated by adding the percentage of each completed and current (within sustainment interval) E-Coded training event. The percentage for each MET is calculated the same way and all are added together and divided by the number of METS to determine unit CRP. For ease of calculation, we will say that each MET has 4 E-Coded events, each contributing 25% towards the completion of the MET. If the unit has completed and is current on three of the four E-Coded events for a given MET, then they have completed 75% of the MET. The CRP for each MET is added together and divided by the number of METS to get unit CRP; unit CRP is the average of MET CRP.

For Example:

        MET 1:   75% complete   (3 of 4 E-Coded events trained)
        MET 2: 100% complete   (6 of 6 E-Coded events trained)
        MET 3:   25% complete   (1 of 4 E-Coded events trained)
        MET 4:   50% complete   (2 of 4 E-Coded events trained)
        MET 5:   75% complete   (3 of 4 E-Coded events trained)

To get unit CRP, simply add the CRP for each MET and divide by the number of METS:

        MET CRP: 75 + 100 + 25 + 50 + 75 = 325

        Unit CRP: 325 (total MET CRP)/5 (total number of METS) = 65%

1009. T&R EVENT COMPOSITION

1. This section explains each of the components of a T&R event. These items are included in all events in each T&R Manual.

    a. Event Code (see Sect 1006). The event code is a 4-4-4 character set. For individual training events, the first 4 characters indicate the occupational function. The second 4 characters indicate functional area (TAC, CBTS, VOPS, etc.). The third 4 characters are simply a numerical designator for the event.

    b. Event Title. The event title is the name of the event.

    c. E-Coded. This is a "yes/no" category to indicate whether or not the event is E-Coded. If yes, the event contributes toward the CRP of the associated MET. The value of each E-Coded event is based on number of E-Coded events for that MET. Refer to paragraph 1008 for detailed explanation of E-Coded events.

    d. Supported MET(s). List all METs that are supported by the training event.

    e. Sustainment Interval. This is the period, expressed in number of months, between evaluation and retraining requirements. Skills and capabilities acquired through the accomplishment of training events are refreshed at pre-determined intervals. It is essential that these intervals are adhered to in order to ensure Marines maintain proficiency.

    f. Billet. Individual training events may contain a list of billets within the community that are responsible for performing that event. This ensures that the billet's expected tasks are clearly articulated and a Marine's readiness to perform in that billet is measured.

    g. Grade. Each individual training event will list the rank(s) at which Marines are required to learn and sustain the training event.

    h. Initial Training Setting. For Individual T&R Events only, this specifies the location for initial instruction of the training event in one of three categories (formal school, managed on-the-job training, distance learning). Regardless of the specified Initial Training Setting, any T&R event may be introduced and evaluated during managed on-the-job training.

(1) "FORMAL" - When the Initial Training Setting of an event is identified as "FORMAL" (formal school), the appropriate formal school or training detachment is required to provide initial training in the event. Conversely, formal schools and training detachments are not authorized to provide training in events designated as Initial Training Setting "MOJT" or "DL." Since the duration of formal school training must be constrained to optimize Operating Forces' manning, this element provides the mechanism for Operating Forces' prioritization of training requirements for both entry-level (1000-level) and career-level (2000-level) T&R Events. For formal schools and training detachments, this element defines the requirements for content of courses.

(2) "DL" - Identifies the training event as a candidate for initial training via a Distance Learning product (correspondence course or MarineNet course).

(3) "MOJT" - Events specified for Managed On-the-Job Training are to be introduced to Marines, and evaluated, as part of training within a unit by supervisory personnel.

i. Event Description. Provide a description of the event purpose, objectives, goals, and requirements. It is a general description of an action requiring learned skills and knowledge (e.g. Camouflage the M1A1 Tank).

j. Condition. Describe the condition(s), under which tasks are performed. Conditions are based on a "real world" operational environment. They indicate what is provided (equipment, materials, manuals, aids, etc.), environmental constraints, conditions under which the task is performed, and any specific cues or indicators to which the performer must respond. When resources or safety requirements limit the conditions, this is stated.

k. Standard. The standard indicates the basis for judging effectiveness of the performance. It consists of a carefully worded statement that identifies the proficiency level expected when the task is performed. The standard provides the minimum acceptable performance parameters and is strictly adhered to. The standard for collective events is general, describing the desired end-state or purpose of the event. While the standard for individual events specifically describe to what proficiency level in terms of accuracy, speed, sequencing, quality of performance, adherence to procedural guidelines, etc., the event is accomplished.

l. Event Components. Describe the actions composing the event and help the user determine what must be accomplished and to properly plan for the event.

m. Prerequisite Events. Prerequisites are academic training or other T&R events that must be completed prior to attempting the task. They are lower-level events or tasks that give the individual/unit the skills required to accomplish the event. They can also be planning steps, administrative requirements, or specific parameters that build toward mission accomplishment.

n. Chained Events. Collective T&R events are supported by lower-level collective and individual T&R events. This enables unit leaders to effectively identify subordinate T&R events that ultimately support specific mission essential tasks. When the accomplishment of any upper-level events, by their nature, result in the performance of certain subordinate and related events, the events are "chained." The completion of chained events will update sustainment interval credit (and CRP for E-Coded events) for the related subordinate level events.

o. Related Events. Provide a list of all Individual Training Standards that support the event.

p. References. The training references are utilized to determine task performance steps, grading criteria, and ensure standardization of training procedures. They assist the trainee in satisfying the performance standards, or the trainer in evaluating the effectiveness of task completion. References are also important to the development of detailed training plans.

q. Distance Learning Products (IMI, CBT, MCI, etc.). Include this component when the event can be taught via one of these media methods vice attending a formal course of instruction or receiving MOJT.

r. Support Requirements. This is a list of the external and internal support the unit and Marines will need to complete the event. The list includes, but is not limited to:

- Range(s)/Training Area
- Ordnance
- Equipment
- Materials
- Other Units/Personnel
- Other Support Requirements

s. Miscellaneous. Provide any additional information that assists in the planning and execution of the event. Miscellaneous information may include, but is not limited to:

- Admin Instructions
- Special Personnel Certifications
- Equipment Operating Hours
- Road Miles

2. Community-based T&R Manuals have several additional components not found in unit-based T&R Manuals. These additions do not apply to this T&R Manual.

1010. CBRN TRAINING

1. All personnel assigned to the operating force must be trained in chemical, biological, radiological, and nuclear defense (CBRN), in order to survive and continue their mission in this environment. Individual proficiency standards are defined as survival and basic operating standards. Survival standards are those that the individual must master in order to survive CBRN attacks. Basic operating standards are those that the

individual, and collectively the unit, must perform to continue operations in a CBRN environment.

2. In order to develop and maintain the ability to operate in a CBRN environment, CBRN training is an integral part of the training plan and events in this T&R Manual. CBRN officers and specialists are instrumental in integrating realistic scenarios/situations that challenge a unit's ability to operate in a CBRN environment. Units should train under CBRN conditions whenever possible. Per reference (c), all units must be capable of accomplishing their assigned mission in a contaminated environment.

1011. NIGHT TRAINING

1. While it is understood that all personnel and units of the operating force are capable of performing their assigned mission in "every climate and place," current doctrine emphasizes the requirement to perform assigned missions at night and during periods of limited visibility. Basic skills are significantly more difficult when visibility is limited.

2. To ensure units are capable of accomplishing their mission they must train under the conditions of limited visibility. Units should strive to conduct all events in this T&R Manual during both day and night/limited visibility conditions. When there is limited training time available, night training should take precedence over daylight training, contingent on individual, crew, and unit proficiency.

1012. OPERATIONAL RISK MANAGEMENT (ORM)

1. ORM is a process that enables commanders to plan for and minimize risk while still accomplishing the mission. It is a decision making tool used by Marines at all levels to increase operational effectiveness by anticipating hazards and reducing the potential for loss, thereby increasing the probability of a successful mission. ORM minimizes risks to acceptable levels, commensurate with mission accomplishment.

2. Commanders, leaders, maintainers, planners, and schedulers will integrate risk assessment in the decision-making process and implement hazard controls to reduce risk to acceptable levels. Applying the ORM process will reduce mishaps, lower costs, and provide for more efficient use of resources. ORM assists the commander in conserving lives and resources and avoiding unnecessary risk, making an informed decision to implement a course of action (COA), identifying feasible and effective control measures where specific measures do not exist, and providing reasonable alternatives for mission accomplishment. Most importantly, ORM assists the commander in determining the balance between training realism and unnecessary risks in training, the impact of training operations on the environment, and the adjustment of training plans to fit the level of proficiency and experience of Sailors/Marines and leaders. Further guidance for ORM is found in references (b) and (d).

1013. APPLICATION OF SIMULATION

1. Simulations/Simulators and other training devices shall be used when they are capable of effectively and economically supplementing training on the identified training task. Particular emphasis shall be placed on simulators that provide training that might be limited by safety considerations or constraints on training space, time, or other resources. When deciding on simulation issues, the primary consideration shall be improving the quality of training and consequently the state of readiness. Potential savings in operating and support costs normally shall be an important secondary consideration.

2. Each training event contains information relating to the applicability of simulation. If simulator training applies to the event, then the applicable simulator(s) is/are listed in the "Simulation" section and the CRP for simulation training is given. This simulation training can either be used in place of live training, at the reduced CRP indicated; or can be used as a precursor training for the live event, i.e., weapons simulators, convoy trainers, observed fire trainers, etc. It is recommended that tasks be performed by simulation prior to being performed in a live-fire environment. However, in the case where simulation is used as a precursor for the live event, then the unit will receive credit for the live event CRP only. If a tactical situation develops that precludes performing the live event, the unit would then receive credit for the simulation CRP.

1014. MARINE CORPS GROUND T&R PROGRAM

1. The Marine Corps Ground T&R Program continues to evolve. The vision for Ground T&R Program is to publish a T&R Manual for every readiness-reporting unit so that core capability METs are clearly defined with supporting collective training standards, and to publish community-based T&R Manuals for all occupational fields whose personnel augment other units to increase their combat and/or logistic capabilities. The vision for this program includes plans to provide a Marine Corps training management information system that enables tracking of unit and individual training accomplishments by unit commanders and small unit leaders, automatically computing CRP for both units and individual Marines based upon MOS and rank (or billet). Linkage of T&R Events to the Marine Corps Task List (MCTL), through the core capability METs, has enabled objective assessment of training readiness in the DRRS.

2. DRRS measures and reports on the readiness of military forces and the supporting infrastructure to meet missions and goals assigned by the Secretary of Defense. With unit CRP based on the unit's training toward its METs, the CRP will provide a more accurate picture of a unit's readiness. This will give fidelity to future funding requests and factor into the allocation of resources. Additionally, the Ground T&R Program will help to ensure training remains focused on mission accomplishment and that training readiness reporting is tied to units' METLs.

CHAPTER 2

MISSION ESSENTIAL TASKS MATRIX

This Chapter is reserve for future use

C2 T&R MANUAL

CHAPTER 3

C2 COLLECTIVE EVENTS

CHAPTER 3

C2 COLLECTIVE EVENTS

3000. PURPOSE. This chapter contains collective training events for Command and Control (C2).

3001. EVENT CODING. Events in the T&R Manual are depicted with a 12 field alphanumeric system, i.e. XXXX-XXXX-XXXX. This chapter utilizes the following methodology:

a. Field one - Each event starts with "C2OP" indicating that the event is for units performing Command and Control.

b. Field two - This field is alpha characters indicating a functional area. Functional areas used at the Battalion level are:

OPS - Operations

c. Field three - This field provides unit level at which the event is accomplished and numerical sequencing.

3002. ADMINISTRATIVE NOTES

1. Commanders should select which Battalion and/or Company collective events= under a MET will be E-Coded for purposes of recording and calculating Combat Readiness Percentages.

2. Each event contains a paragraph that describes internal and external Support Requirements the unit and Marines will need to complete the event. Ranges/Training Areas are described in this section with plain-language description. They are also described using the Range/Facility Codes that identify the type of range and/or training area needed to accomplish the Event. Marines can use the codes to find information about available ranges at their geographic location by using the web-based Range/Training Area Management System (see TECOM website). Ultimate use of the Range/Training Area Code is to relate ranges to readiness by identifying those events that cannot be accomplished at a certain location due to lack of ranges.

3003. INDEX OF EVENTS BY FUNCTIONAL AREA

EVENT	DESCRIPTION	PAGE
C2OP-OPS-4601	Plan for operations	
C2OP-OPS-4602	Conduct assessment	
C2OP-OPS-4603	Conduct Information Management	
C2OP-OPS-4701	Plan for Operations	
C2OP-OPS-4702	Conduct Assessment	
C2OP-OPS-4703	Integrate Joint, Interagency, Intergovernmental, Multinational (JIIM) support into operations	
C2OP-OPS-4704	Conduct Information Management	
C2OP-OPS-5701	Conduct command post operations	
C2OP-OPS-5702	Displace a Command Post (CP)	
C2OP-OPS-5703	Conduct COC operations	
C2OP-OPS-5801	Plan for Operations	
C2OP-OPS-5802	Conduct Assessment	
C2OP-OPS-5803	Integrate Joint, Interagency, Intergovernmental, Multinational (JIIM) support into operations	
C2OP-OPS-5804	Conduct Information Management	
C2OP-OPS-6001	Employ command and control systems	
C2OP-OPS-6002	Establish command and control of an operation	
C2OP-OPS-6003	Execute command and control of an operation	
C2OP-OPS-6004	Conduct Force Deployment Planning & Execution (FDP&E)	
C2OP-OPS-6005	Prepare for Combat Operations	
C2OP-OPS-6801	Conduct command post operations	
C2OP-OPS-6802	Displace a Command Post (CP)	
C2OP-OPS-6803	Conduct COC operations	
C2OP-OPS-7001	Employ command and control systems	
C2OP-OPS-7002	Establish command and control of an operation	
C2OP-OPS-7003	Execute command and control of an operation	
C2OP-OPS-7004	Integrate C2 Systems	
C2OP-OPS-7005	Conduct Force Deployment Planning & Execution (FDP&E)	
C2OP-OPS-8001	Employ command and control systems	
C2OP-OPS-8002	Establish command and control of an operation	
C2OP-OPS-8003	Execute command and control of an operation	
C2OP-OPS-8004	Integrate C2 Systems	
C2OP-OPS-8005	Conduct Force Deployment Planning & Execution (FDP&E)	

3004. 4000-LEVEL EVENTS

C2OP-OPS-4601: Plan for operations

SUPPORTED MET(S): None

EVALUATION-CODED: NO   **SUSTAINMENT INTERVAL:** 12 months

DESCRIPTION: The process that develops an order to direct actions and focus subordinate activities toward accomplishing the mission.

CONDITION: Given Commanders Guidance, key leaders and higher headquarters operations order.

STANDARD: To communicate the commander's intent, guidance, and decisions in a clear, useful form that is easily understood by those who must execute the order.

EVENT COMPONENTS:
1. Conduct Problem Framing.
2. Determine planning process (MCPP, R2P2, Hasty Planning, or other method).
3. Determine Time Available.
4. Establish timeline for planning and preparation.
5. Issue Warning Order.
6. Implement Cultural Considerations into Mission Planning.
7. Create orders (OPORD, FRAGO, Decision Support Tools, etc).
8. Issue orders.
9. Implement feedback mechanisms.
10. Coordinate planning with higher, adjacent, subordinate, and supporting units.

C2OP-OPS-4602: Conduct assessment

SUPPORTED MET(S): None

EVALUATION-CODED: NO   **SUSTAINMENT INTERVAL:** 12 months

DESCRIPTION: Commanders and Key leaders monitor measures of effectiveness and measures of performance to achieve articulated endstate.

CONDITION: Given Commanders Guidance, higher headquarters operations order, and Key leaders.

STANDARD: To allow the commander to assess mission effectiveness IOT support the decision-making process.

EVENT COMPONENTS:
1. Develop Information Requirements for MOE & MOP.
2. Determine IRs for collection.
3. Develop a collections plan (internal & external).
4. Develop an IR tracking method.
5. Determine objectives (Campaign, Mission, Phases, LOOs, etc.).

6. Establish endstates.
7. Establish conditions & subconditions, as necessary.
8. Develop Measure of Effectiveness.
9. Develop Measures of Performance.

C2OP-OPS-4603: Conduct Information Management

SUPPORTED MET(S): None

EVALUATION-CODED: NO   **SUSTAINMENT INTERVAL:** 12 months

CONDITION: Given Commanders Guidance, operations order, Key leaders, Unit TO&E, functional communications architecture and integrated C2 systems.

STANDARD: To facilitate the commander's decision making process.

EVENT COMPONENTS:
1. Identify Decision Points.
2. Identify other information exchange requirements (IERS).
3. Identify people, relationships & organizations that affect information flow.
4. Execute Information protocols.
5. Process information (refine and sort).
6. Analyze necessary information (analyze, fuse and share).
7. Create quality information.
8. Collate quality information for CO and key leaders to make decisions IAW levels of authority.
9. Disseminate decisions to higher, adjacent, supporting elements.
10. Integrate with B2C2WGs inputs, processes and outputs to support the units decision making [Boards, Bureaus, Cells, Committees, and Working Groups].
11. Ensure decision makers have access to necessary information at the right time/place.
12. Store Information.
13. Conduct scheduled and unscheduled inspections of stored.
14. Assess the IM plan. (as required)
15. Modify the plan. (as required)
16. Establish a Common Tactical Picture (CTP).

C2OP-OPS-4701: Plan for Operations

SUPPORTED MET(S): None

EVALUATION-CODED: NO   **SUSTAINMENT INTERVAL:** 1 month

DESCRIPTION: The process that develops an order to direct actions and focus subordinate activities toward accomplishing the mission.

CONDITION: Given Commanders Guidance, higher headquarters operations order and battle staff.

STANDARD: To communicate the commander's intent, guidance, and decisions in a clear, useful form that is easily understood by those who must execute the order.

EVENT COMPONENTS:
1. Conduct Problem Framing.
2. Determine planning process (Campaign, MCPP, R2P2, Hasty Planning, or other method).
3. Determine Time Available.
4. Establish timeline for planning and preparation.
5. Issue Warning Order.
6. Conduct OPT.
7. Implement Cultural Considerations into Mission Planning.
8. Create orders (OPORD, FRAGO, Decision Support Tools, etc).
9. Issue orders.
10. Implement feedback mechanisms.
11. Coordinate planning with higher, adjacent, subordinate, and supporting units.

C2OP-OPS-4702: Conduct Assessment

SUPPORTED MET(S): None

EVALUATION-CODED: NO   **SUSTAINMENT INTERVAL:** 1 month

DESCRIPTION: Commanders and battle staff monitor measures of effectiveness and measures of performance to achieve articulated endstates.

CONDITION: Given Commanders Guidance, operations order, battle staff, and Joint, Interagency Intergovernmental Multinational Organizations.

STANDARD: To allow the commander to assess mission effectiveness IOT support the decision-making process.

EVENT COMPONENTS:
1. Determine the purpose of the campaign or operation.
2. Determine objectives (Campaign, Mission, Phases, LOOs, etc.).
3. Establish Endstates.
4. Establish conditions & subconditions. (as required)
5. Develop Measures of Effectiveness.
6. Develop Measures of Performance.
7. Develop Information Requirements for MOE & MOP.
8. Determine IRs for collection.
9. Develop a collections plan (internal & external).
10. Develop an IR tracking method.
11. Develop IR analysis method.
12. Integrate IR analysis into the unit Battle Rhythm.
13. Compare IR to MOE & MOP.
14. Develop recommended actions and/or decisions.
15. Track actions & decisions.
16. Modify MOE, MOP and analysis tools. (as required)
17. Integrate Objectives.

C2OP-OPS-4703: Integrate Joint, Interagency, Intergovernmental, Multinational (JIIM) support into operations

SUPPORTED MET(S): None

EVALUATION-CODED: NO   **SUSTAINMENT INTERVAL:** 1 month

CONDITION: Given Higher Headquarters operations order, Commanders Guidance, Commanders Battle space Area Evaluation (CBAE), battle staff, Unit TO&E, functional communications architecture and integrated C2 systems.

STANDARD: To achieve unity of effort and bring all relevant assets to bear on the situation.

EVENT COMPONENTS:
1. Identify capabilities limitations and shortfalls from staff assessments.
2. Identify existing JIIM organizations in your AO, AI and AoI.
3. Synchronize goals, tasks, capabilities, limitation, key leaders and Command/Support relationships.
4. Identify JIIM organizational gaps.
5. Coordinate the support of JIIM.
6. Identify security and planning requirements for JIIM.
7. Verify unity of effort/purpose.
8. Assess unity of effort/purpose.

C2OP-OPS-4704: Conduct Information Management

SUPPORTED MET(S): None

EVALUATION-CODED: NO   **SUSTAINMENT INTERVAL:** 1 month

CONDITION: Given Commanders Guidance, operations order, battle staff, Unit TO&E, functional communications architecture and integrated C2 systems.

STANDARD: To facilitate the commander's decision making process.

EVENT COMPONENTS:
1. Identify other information exchange requirements (IERS).
2. Identify people, relationships & organizations that affect information flow.
3. Execute Information protocols.
4. Process information (refine and sort).
5. Analyze necessary information (analyze, fuse and share).
6. Identify Decision Points.
7. Create quality information.
8. Collate quality information.
9. Disseminate decisions to higher, adjacent, supporting elements.
10. Modify B2C2WGs inputs, processes and outputs to support the units decision making (Boards, Bureaus, Cells, Committees, and Working Groups).
11. Store Information.
12. Conduct scheduled and unscheduled inspections of stored materials.
13. Assess the IM plan. (as required)

14. Modify the plan. (as required)
15. Establish a Common Tactical Picture (CTP).

3005. 5000-LEVEL EVENTS

C2OP-OPS-5701: Conduct command post operations

SUPPORTED MET(S): None

EVALUATION-CODED: NO   **SUSTAINMENT INTERVAL:** 12 months

CONDITION: Given supporting attachments, an operations order and commander's guidance.

STANDARD: To integrate systems, personnel and processes to execute command and control of operations.

EVENT COMPONENTS:
1. Establish communication with higher, adjacent and subordinate units.
2. Conduct information management.
3. Create procedures to transition control to appropriate echelons.
4. Maintain continuity of operations.
5. Establish fire support coordination center.
6. Establish systems control.
7. Organize staff sections for forward, main and rear.
8. Establish intelligence operations center.
9. Establish administration and logistics operations center.
10. Establish Combat operations center.

REFERENCES:
1. DCOCSOP Digital COC SOP for Battalion Operations in Irregular Warfare
2. MCWP 3-1 Ground Combat Operations
3. MCWP 3-16 Fire Support Coordination in the Ground Combat Element
4. MCWP 5-1 Marine Corps Planning Process (MCPP)

C2OP-OPS-5702: Displace a Command Post (CP)

SUPPORTED MET(S): None

EVALUATION-CODED: NO   **SUSTAINMENT INTERVAL:** 12 months

DESCRIPTION: This event requires the unit staff to exercise command and control of operations while displacing forward, main, and rear CPs through the area of operations, despite the challenges posed by the condition on embarkation, communications, and other functions.

CONDITION: Given supporting attachments, displacement procedures, operations order and commander's guidance.

STANDARD: To transfer command and control of operations among various CPs while maneuvering through the area of operations.

EVENT COMPONENTS:
1. Conduct a site survey.
2. Implement methods of embarkation/transportation.

3. Transfer authority to an alternate CP.
4. Establish CP.
5. Conduct Command Post Operations.
6. Reassume authority at the CP.
7. Establish protocol for the transfer of authority.
8. Establish protocols/procedures that mitigate the losses of communications and situational awareness.

REFERENCES:
1. MCDP 6 Command and Control
2. MCWP 5-1 Marine Corps Planning Process (MCPP)

SUPPORT REQUIREMENTS:

RANGE/TRAINING AREA: Facility Code 17410 Maneuver/Training Area, Light Forces

---

C2OP-OPS-5703: Conduct COC operations

SUPPORTED MET(S): None

EVALUATION-CODED: NO   **SUSTAINMENT INTERVAL:** 12 months

DESCRIPTION: The COC is the location where the aggregation and dissemination of information provides the commander and staff with situational awareness which facilitates the decision making process.

CONDITION: Given an operations order, current unit TO&E and battle staff, communication assets and C2 systems.

STANDARD: To integrate systems, personnel and processes to execute command and control of operations.

EVENT COMPONENTS:
1. Organize battle staff. (Warfighting Functions)
2. Establish a COC.
3. Establish COC watch.
4. Maintain battle rhythm.
5. Coordinate movement of forces.
6. Execute Information Management procedures.
7. Conduct battle drills.
8. Maintain communications with HAS units.
9. Maintain CTP.
10. Conduct cross boundary coordination.
11. Synchronize staff section operations.

REFERENCES:
1. DCOCSOP Digital COC SOP for Battalion Operations in Irregular Warfare
2. MCWP 1-0 Marine Corps Operations
3. MCWP 2-1 Intelligence Operations
4. MCWP 3-1 Ground Combat Operations
5. MCWP 4_1 LOGISTICS OPERATIONS

6. MCWP 5-1 Marine Corps Planning Process (MCPP)
7. MCWP 6-2 MAGTF Command and Control Operations

C2OP-OPS-5801: Plan for Operations

SUPPORTED MET(S): None

EVALUATION-CODED: NO   **SUSTAINMENT INTERVAL:** 1 month

DESCRIPTION: The process that develops an order to direct actions and focus subordinate activities toward accomplishing the mission.

CONDITION: Given Commanders Guidance, higher headquarters operations order and battle staff.

STANDARD: To communicate the commander's intent, guidance, and decisions in a clear, useful form that is easily understood by those who must execute the order.

EVENT COMPONENTS:
1. Conduct Problem Framing.
2. Determine planning process (Campaign, MCPP, R2P2, Hasty Planning, or other method).
3. Determine Time Available.
4. Establish timeline for planning and preparation.
5. Issue Warning Order.
6. Conduct OPT.
7. Implement Cultural Considerations into Mission Planning.
8. Create orders (OPORD, FRAGO, Decision Support Tools, etc).
9. Issue orders.
10. Implement feedback mechanisms.
11. Coordinate planning with higher, adjacent, subordinate, and supporting units.

C2OP-OPS-5802: Conduct Assessment

SUPPORTED MET(S): None

EVALUATION-CODED: NO   **SUSTAINMENT INTERVAL:** 1 month

DESCRIPTION: Commanders and battle staff monitor measures of effectiveness and measures of performance to achieve articulated endstates.

CONDITION: Given Commanders Guidance, operations order, battle staff, and Joint, Interagency Intergovernmental Multinational Organizations.

STANDARD: To allow the commander to assess mission effectiveness in order to support the decision-making process.

EVENT COMPONENTS:
1. Determine IRs for collection.

2. Develop a collections plan (internal & external).
3. Develop an IR tracking method.
4. Develop IR analysis method.
5. Integrate IR analysis into the unit Battle Rhythm.
6. Compare IR to MOE & MOP.
7. Develop recommended actions and/or decisions.
8. Track actions & decisions.
9. Modify MOE, MOP and analysis tools. (as required)
10. Integrate Objectives.
11. Determine the purpose of the campaign or operation.
12. Determine objectives (Campaign, Mission, Phases, LOOs, etc.).
13. Establish Endstates.
14. Establish conditions & subconditions. (as required)
15. Develop Measures of Effectiveness.
16. Develop Measures of Performance.
17. Develop Information Requirements for MOE & MOP.

C2OP-OPS-5803: Integrate Joint, Interagency, Intergovernmental, Multinational (JIIM) support into operations

SUPPORTED MET(S): None

EVALUATION-CODED: NO   **SUSTAINMENT INTERVAL:** 1 month

CONDITION: Given Higher Headquarters operations order, Commanders Guidance, Commanders Battle space Area Evaluation (CBAE), battle staff, Unit TO&E, functional communications architecture and integrated C2 systems.

STANDARD: To achieve unity of effort and bring all relevant assets to bear on the situation.

EVENT COMPONENTS:
1. Identify capabilities limitations and shortfalls from staff assessments.
2. Identify existing JIIM organizations in your AO, AI and AoI.
3. Synchronize goals, tasks, capabilities, limitation, key leaders and Command/Support relationships.
4. Identify JIIM organizational gaps.
5. Coordinate the support of JIIM.
6. Identify security and planning requirements for JIIM.
7. Verify unity of effort/purpose.
8. Assess unity of effort/purpose.

C2OP-OPS-5804: Conduct Information Management

SUPPORTED MET(S): None

EVALUATION-CODED: NO   **SUSTAINMENT INTERVAL:** 1 month

CONDITION: Given Commanders Guidance, operations order, battle staff, Unit TO&E, functional communications architecture and integrated C2 systems.

STANDARD: To facilitate the commander's decision making process.

EVENT COMPONENTS:
1. Identify Decision Points.
2. Identify other information exchange requirements (IERS).
3. Identify people, relationships & organizations that affect information flow.
4. Execute Information protocols.
5. Process information (refine and sort).
6. Analyze necessary information (analyze, fuse and share).
7. Create quality information.
8. Collate quality information.
9. Disseminate decisions to higher, adjacent, supporting elements.
10. Modify B2C2WGs inputs, processes and outputs to support the units decision making [Boards, Bureaus, Cells, Committees, and Working Groups].
11. Store Information.
12. Conduct scheduled and unscheduled inspections of stored materials.
13. Assess the IM plan. (as required)
14. Modify the plan. (as required)
15. Establish a Common Tactical Picture (CTP).

3006. 6000-LEVEL EVENTS

C2OP-OPS-6001: Employ command and control systems

SUPPORTED MET(S): None

EVALUATION-CODED: NO   **SUSTAINMENT INTERVAL:** 12 months

DESCRIPTION: Units must be able to employ C2 systems to support the commander and the units overall mission. When used effectively, C2 systems enhance the units ability to execute C2 and provide the commander and staff with situational awareness.

CONDITION: Given an operations order, unit TO&E, functional communications architecture.

STANDARD: To maintain situational awareness of the unit and relevant organizations; and rapidly promulgate decisions and vital information.

EVENT COMPONENTS:
1. Identify C2 systems requirements to higher HQ.
2. Plan C2 systems implementation.
3. Implement C2 systems.
4. Rehearse C2 Systems interactions.
5. Maintain C2 systems.
6. Maintain a Common Tactical Picture.

REFERENCES:
1. DCOCSOP Digital COC SOP for Battalion Operations in Irregular Warfare
2. MCO 3500.26A Universal Naval Task List (UNTL) Version 3.0 (Jan 07)
3. MCO 3500.27_ Operational Risk Management (ORM)
4. MCWP 1-0 Marine Corps Operations
5. MCWP 2-1 Intelligence Operations
6. MCWP 3-1 Ground Combat Operations
7. MCWP 4_1 LOGISTICS OPERATIONS
8. MCWP 5-1 Marine Corps Planning Process (MCPP)
9. MCWP 6-2 MAGTF Command and Control Operations

C2OP-OPS-6004: Conduct Force Deployment Planning & Execution (FDP&E)

SUPPORTED MET(S): None

EVALUATION-CODED: NO   **SUSTAINMENT INTERVAL:** 12 months

DESCRIPTION: The FDP&E process outlines the detailed planning and execution timeline, force deployment planning guidelines, logistics and force sustainment, manpower planning guidelines and Global Force Management Process.

CONDITION: Given warning order, Commanders Guidance, key leaders, Unit TO&E, functional communications architecture and integrated C2 systems.

STANDARD: To ensure the unit supports the operational plan by arriving at the correct location, properly equipped and prepared for combat operations.

EVENT COMPONENTS:
1. Identify key leader's responsibilities.
2. Conduct operational planning.
3. Assess relevant planning factors (manifest due dates, inspections schedule, etc).
4. Identify transportation requirements.
5. Prepare Unit Manifest.
6. Prepare Unit Equipment Density Lists (EDLs).
7. Report TPFDD requirements to higher headquarters.
8. Disseminate a movement schedule.
9. Supervise embarkation/movement to staging area.
10. Conduct inspections.
11. Disseminate the plan for RSO&I.
12. Execute the force flow plan.

C2OP-OPS-6005: Prepare for Combat Operations

SUPPORTED MET(S): None

EVALUATION-CODED: NO   SUSTAINMENT INTERVAL: 12 months

CONDITION: Given an operations order or warning order.

STANDARD: In order to successfully accomplish the tasks/mission and satisfy commander's intent.

EVENT COMPONENTS:
1. Conduct Planning.
2. Arrange for reconnaissance.
3. Conduct Reconnaissance.
4. Conduct necessary coordination with higher, adjacent, subordinate, supporting units.
5. Issue orders.
6. Supervise.
7. Perform pre-combat inspections (PCIs).
8. Perform pre-combat checks (PCCs).
9. Modify the plan based off changes to METT-T, other units actions, and/or issues identified during rehearsals, inspections, checks, etc.

C2OP-OPS-6801: Conduct command post operations

SUPPORTED MET(S): None

EVALUATION-CODED: NO   SUSTAINMENT INTERVAL: 12 months

CONDITION: Given supporting attachments, an operations order and commander's guidance.

STANDARD: To integrate systems, personnel and processes to execute command and control of operations.

EVENT COMPONENTS:
1. Establish procedures to conduct movement of CP (Support Functions).
2. Establish communication with higher, adjacent and subordinate units.
3. Conduct information management.
4. Create procedures to transition control to appropriate echelons.
5. Establish displacement procedures.
6. Maintain continuity of operations.
7. Maintain command and control during displacement.
8. Establish fire support coordination center.
9. Establish systems control.
10. Organize staff sections for forward, main and rear.
11. Establish intelligence operations center.
12. Establish administration and logistics operations center.
13. Establish Combat operations center.

REFERENCES:
1. DCOCSOP Digital COC SOP for Battalion Operations in Irregular Warfare
2. MCWP 3-1 Ground Combat Operations
3. MCWP 3-16 Fire Support Coordination in the Ground Combat Element
4. MCWP 5-1 Marine Corps Planning Process (MCPP)

C2OP-OPS-6802: Displace a Command Post (CP)

SUPPORTED MET(S): None

EVALUATION-CODED: NO   **SUSTAINMENT INTERVAL:** 12 months

DESCRIPTION: This event requires the unit staff to exercise command and control of operations while displacing forward, main, and rear CPs through the area of operations, despite the challenges posed by the condition on embarkation, communications, and other functions.

CONDITION: Given supporting attachments, operations order and commander's guidance.

STANDARD: To transfer command and control of operations among various CPs while maneuvering through the area of operations.

EVENT COMPONENTS:
1. Conduct a site survey.
2. Implement methods of embarkation/transportation.
3. Transfer authority to an alternate CP.
4. Establish CP.
5. Conduct Command Post Operations.
6. Reassume authority at the CP.
7. Establish protocol for the transfer of authority.
8. Establish protocols/procedures that mitigate the losses of communications and situational awareness.

REFERENCES:
1. MCDP 6 Command and Control
2. MCWP 5-1 Marine Corps Planning Process (MCPP)

SUPPORT REQUIREMENTS:

RANGE/TRAINING AREA: Facility Code 17410 Maneuver/Training Area, Light Forces

---

C2OP-OPS-6803: Conduct COC operations

SUPPORTED MET(S): None

EVALUATION-CODED: NO   SUSTAINMENT INTERVAL: 12 months

DESCRIPTION: The COC is the location where the aggregation and dissemination of information provides the commander and staff with situational awareness which facilitates the decision making process.

CONDITION: Given an operations order, current unit TO&E and battle staff, communication assets and C2 systems.

STANDARD: To integrate systems, personnel and processes to execute command and control of operations.

EVENT COMPONENTS:
1. Organize battle staff. (Warfighting Functions)
2. Establish a COC.
3. Establish COC watch.
4. Maintain battle rhythm.
5. Coordinate movement of forces.
6. Execute Information Management procedures.
7. Conduct battle drills.
8. Maintain communications with HAS units.
9. Maintain CTP.
10. Conduct cross boundary coordination.
11. Synchronize staff section operations.

REFERENCES:
1. DCOCSOP Digital COC SOP for Battalion Operations in Irregular Warfare
2. MCWP 1-0 Marine Corps Operations
3. MCWP 2-1 Intelligence Operations
4. MCWP 3-1 Ground Combat Operations
5. MCWP 4_1 LOGISTICS OPERATIONS
6. MCWP 5-1 Marine Corps Planning Process (MCPP)
7. MCWP 6-2 MAGTF Command and Control Operations

3007. 7000-LEVEL EVENTS

C2OP-OPS-7001: Employ command and control systems

SUPPORTED MET(S): None

EVALUATION-CODED: NO   **SUSTAINMENT INTERVAL**: 12 months

DESCRIPTION: Units must be able to employ C2 systems to support the commander and the units overall mission. When used effectively, C2 systems will enhance the unit's ability to execute C2 and provides the commander and staff with situational awareness.

CONDITION: Given an operations order, operational COC, battle staff, and functional communications architecture.

STANDARD: To maintain situational awareness of the unit and relevant organizations; and rapidly promulgate decisions and vital information.

EVENT COMPONENTS:
1. Prepare C2 systems access requests.
2. Implement C2 systems architecture.
3. Rehearse C2 Systems interactions.
4. Maintain C2 systems architecture.
5. Maintain a Common Tactical Picture.
6. Plan C2 systems architecture.
7. Design C2 systems architecture.

REFERENCES:
1. DCOCSOP Digital COC SOP for Battalion Operations in Irregular Warfare
2. MCO 3500.26A Universal Naval Task List (UNTL) Version 3.0 (Jan 07)
3. MCO 3500.27_ Operational Risk Management (ORM)
4. MCWP 1-0 Marine Corps Operations
5. MCWP 2-1 Intelligence Operations
6. MCWP 3-1 Ground Combat Operations
7. MCWP 4_1 LOGISTICS OPERATIONS
8. MCWP 5-1 Marine Corps Planning Process (MCPP)
9. MCWP 6-2 MAGTF Command and Control Operations

C2OP-OPS-7004: Integrate C2 Systems

SUPPORTED MET(S): None

EVALUATION-CODED: NO   **SUSTAINMENT INTERVAL**: 1 month

DESCRIPTION: The proper integration of all C2 systems, collaborative tools and processes to include Version Control, Configuration Management, Authority to Operate, Information Assurance are important to the timely decision making abilities of the commander and his staff.

CONDITION: Given an operations order with an Intel systems tab, Maneuver Systems tab, Aviation C2 Systems tab, Fires Systems tab, Logistics Systems tab, Force Protection tab, Collaborative Systems tab, Annex K, Annex U, and functional communications architecture, using current unit TO&E, communication assets and C2 systems.

STANDARD: To ensure C2 systems support the information management plan and mission.

EVENT COMPONENTS:
1. Establish C2 Systems Integration Plan.
2. Produce Annex C, Appendix X, tab X.
3. Employ C2 Systems.

REFERENCES:
1. DCOCSOP Digital COC SOP for Battalion Operations in Irregular Warfare
2. MCWP 1-0 Marine Corps Operations
3. MCWP 2-1 Intelligence Operations
4. MCWP 3-1 Ground Combat Operations
5. MCWP 4_1 LOGISTICS OPERATIONS
6. MCWP 5-1 Marine Corps Planning Process (MCPP)
7. MCWP 6-2 MAGTF Command and Control Operations

C2OP-OPS-7005: Conduct Force Deployment Planning & Execution (FDP&E)

SUPPORTED MET(S): None

EVALUATION-CODED: NO   **SUSTAINMENT INTERVAL:** 1 month

DESCRIPTION: The FDP&E process outlines the detailed planning and execution timeline, force deployment planning guidelines, logistics and force sustainment, manpower planning guidelines and Global Force Management Process.

CONDITION: Given warning order, Commanders Guidance, battle staff, Unit TO&E, functional communications architecture and integrated C2 systems.

STANDARD: To ensure the unit supports the operational plan by arriving at the correct location, properly equipped and prepared for combat operations ISO assigned tasks.

EVENT COMPONENTS:
1. Identify command and staff responsibilities.
2. Conduct operational planning.
3. Assess relevant planning factors.
4. Determine transportation requirements.
5. Prepare Unit Manifest.
6. Prepare Unit Equipment Density Lists (EDLs).
7. Report TPFDD requirements to higher headquarters.
8. Disseminate a movement schedule.
9. Supervise embarkation/movement to staging area.
10. Conduct inspections.
11. Disseminate the plan for RSO&I.
12. Execute the force flow plan.

3008. 8000-LEVEL EVENTS

C2OP-OPS-8001: Employ command and control systems

SUPPORTED MET(S): None

EVALUATION-CODED: NO   **SUSTAINMENT INTERVAL:** 12 months

DESCRIPTION: Units must be able to employ C2 systems to support the commander and the units overall mission. When used effectively, C2 systems will enhance the units ability to execute C2 and provides the commander and staff with situational awareness.

CONDITION: Given an operations order, operational COC, battle staff, and functional communications architecture.

STANDARD: To maintain situational awareness of the unit and relevant organizations; and rapidly promulgate decisions and vital information.

EVENT COMPONENTS:
1. Engineer C2 systems architecture.
2. Prepare C2 systems access requests.
3. Implement C2 systems architecture.
4. Rehearse C2 Systems interactions.
5. Maintain C2 systems architecture.
6. Maintain a Common Tactical Picture.
7. Plan C2 systems architecture.
8. Design C2 systems architecture.

REFERENCES:
1. DCOCSOP Digital COC SOP for Battalion Operations in Irregular Warfare
2. MCO 3500.26A Universal Naval Task List (UNTL) Version 3.0 (Jan 07)
3. MCO 3500.27_ Operational Risk Management (ORM)
4. MCWP 1-0 Marine Corps Operations
5. MCWP 2-1 Intelligence Operations
6. MCWP 3-1 Ground Combat Operations
7. MCWP 4_1 LOGISTICS OPERATIONS
8. MCWP 5-1 Marine Corps Planning Process (MCPP)
9. MCWP 6-2 MAGTF Command and Control Operations

C2OP-OPS-8002: Establish command and control of an operation

SUPPORTED MET(S): None

EVALUATION-CODED: NO   **SUSTAINMENT INTERVAL:** 12 months

DESCRIPTION: The proper preparation for C2 prior to conducting MAGTF operations is imperative to the overall success of the mission.

CONDITION: Given an operations order and a battle staff.

STANDARD: To set the conditions for C2.

EVENT COMPONENTS:
1. Establish the Combat Operations Center.
2. Establish the Command Post. (as required)
3. Install communications architecture.
4. Establish Command & Support relationships.
5. Employ Command and Control Systems.
6. Prepare for operations. (order's issuance, PCCs, PCIs, rehearsals, etc)
7. Assess Annex U methods of delivery.

REFERENCES:
1. MCDP 6 Command and Control
2. MCWP 5-1 Marine Corps Planning Process (MCPP)

C2OP-OPS-8003: Execute command and control of an operation

SUPPORTED MET(S): None

EVALUATION-CODED: NO   **SUSTAINMENT INTERVAL:** 12 months

DESCRIPTION: The proper execution of C2 during all phases of an operation is imperative to the overall success of the mission.

CONDITION: Given an operations order, operational COC and battle staff, and functional communications architecture.

STANDARD: To achieve desired endstates.

EVENT COMPONENTS:
1. Employ C2 Systems.
2. Implement Tactical Control Measures.
3. Track decision points (CCIRs, Essential Elements of Friendly Information EEFI).
4. Track higher, adjacent, supporting units.
5. Provide FRAG orders to subordinate and supporting elements. (as required)
6. Provide information to Higher, Adjacent, and supporting units.
7. Monitor transitions (phases, units, etc).
8. Maintain situational awareness.
9. Prepare for follow on operations as appropriate (branches, sequels, etc).

REFERENCES:
1. DCOCSOP Digital COC SOP for Battalion Operations in Irregular Warfare
2. MCWP 1-0 Marine Corps Operations
3. MCWP 2-1 Intelligence Operations
4. MCWP 3-1 Ground Combat Operations
5. MCWP 3-2 Aviation Operations
6. MCWP 4_1 LOGISTICS OPERATIONS
7. MCWP 5-1 Marine Corps Planning Process (MCPP)
8. MCWP 6-2 MAGTF Command and Control Operations

C2OP-OPS-8004: Integrate C2 Systems

SUPPORTED MET(S): None

EVALUATION-CODED: NO   **SUSTAINMENT INTERVAL:** 1 month

DESCRIPTION: The proper integration of all C2 systems, collaborative tools and processes to include Version Control, Configuration Management, Authority to Operate, Information Assurance are important to the timely decision making abilities of the commander and his staff.

CONDITION: Given an operations order with an Intel systems tab, Maneuver Systems tab, Aviation C2 Systems tab, Fires Systems tab, Logistics Systems tab, Force Protection tab, Collaborative Systems tab, Annex K, Annex U, and functional communications architecture, using current unit TO&E, communication assets and C2 systems.

STANDARD: To ensure C2 systems support the information management plan and mission.

EVENT COMPONENTS:
1. Establish C2 Systems Integration Plan.
2. Produce Annex C, Appendix X, tab X.
3. Employ C2 Systems.

REFERENCES:
1. DCOCSOP Digital COC SOP for Battalion Operations in Irregular Warfare
2. MCWP 1-0 Marine Corps Operations
3. MCWP 2-1 Intelligence Operations
4. MCWP 3-1 Ground Combat Operations
5. MCWP 4_1 LOGISTICS OPERATIONS
6. MCWP 5-1 Marine Corps Planning Process (MCPP)
7. MCWP 6-2 MAGTF Command and Control Operations

C2OP-OPS-8005: Conduct Force Deployment Planning & Execution (FDP&E)

SUPPORTED MET(S): None

EVALUATION-CODED: NO   **SUSTAINMENT INTERVAL:** 1 month

DESCRIPTION: The FDP&E process outlines the detailed planning and execution timeline, force deployment planning guidelines, logistics and force sustainment, manpower planning guidelines and Global Force Management Process.

CONDITION: Given warning order, Commanders Guidance, battle staff, Unit TO&E, functional communications architecture and integrated C2 systems.

STANDARD: To ensure the unit supports the operational plan by arriving at the correct location, properly equipped and prepared for combat operations ISO assigned tasks.

EVENT COMPONENTS:
1. Identify command and staff responsibilities.
2. Conduct operational planning.
3. Assess relevant planning factors.
4. Determine transportation requirements.
5. Prepare Unit Manifest.
6. Prepare Unit Equipment Density Lists (EDLs).
7. Report TPFDD requirements to higher headquarters.
8. Disseminate a movement schedule.
9. Supervise embarkation/movement to staging area.
10. Conduct inspections.
11. Disseminate the plan for RSO&I.
12. Execute the force flow plan.

C2 T&R MANUAL

CHAPTER 4

C2 INDIVIDUAL EVENTS

CHAPTER 4

C2 INDIVIDUAL EVENTS

4000. PURPOSE

1. With the rapid fielding and employment of multiple Command and Control systems, qualified Command and Control systems operators are becoming increasingly critical. These Command and Control systems are found in tactical vehicles as well as in unit COCs. The COC is increasingly supported by automated tactical data systems and data communications. These systems support the information processing and exchange requirements of the COC and enable it to monitor and direct current operations. Recognizing that the vast majority of Command and Control system operators have no associated MOS, it is critical that the Marine Corps provide these operators initial and sustainment training enabling them to perform the duties and responsibilities required of their associated billet. The C2 TECOE provides this Command and Control training through its five MISTCs. They provide "incidental operators" with the needed Command and Control training for those Command and Control systems not associated with an MOS producing school; and they provide Command and Control sustainment training on those Command and Control systems that are associated with an MOS producing school. The MISTCs not only teach the science of Command and Control (technical training), but also the art of Command and Control (integrated and collective training) as well.

2. Preparing Marines to effectively exploit Command and Control systems is the "long pole in the tent" as the Marine Corps develops increasingly integrated Command and Control systems. The human element comprises the most critical aspect of warfare. It is through our Marines that the true art of warfare is exercised. While properly equipping our Marines is essential, effective training is absolutely critical. The most expensive and elaborately constructed technical solution is not a legitimate war fighting capability until a Marine is educated on what the system is intended to do and how to employ that system effectively within the greater unit context. Training and educating Marines, in both the art and the science of MAGTF Command and Control, is a necessity if we are to realize technology's full potential and enhance lethality and effectiveness as we fight across the spectrum of conflict.

3. This manual provides the baseline Command and Control training requirements for individuals operating tactical vehicles as well as those placed in key billets of the COC. Co-locating the staff in one, central location is critical to creating the synergy required among the different staff functions, which enables information sharing among the right people at the right time. All actions of the COC staff collectively support the commander's decision making process. This document will be revised annually to ensure it is both current and relevant to today's warfighter.

4001. EVENT CODING. Events in the T&R Manual are depicted with an up-to-12-field alphanumeric system, i.e. XXXX-XXXX-XXXX. This chapter utilizes the following methodology:

a. Field one – Each event in this chapter begins with "C2OP" indicating that the event is for COC staff.

b. Field two – This field is alpha characters indicating a functional area. Functional areas for COC staff are:

COC – Combat Operations Center   INST – Install
MAIN – Maintain   OPS – Operations
OPER – Operate   PLAN – Planning
IO – Information Operations

c. Field three – This field provides task level and numerical sequencing.

4002. INDEX OF EVENTS BY FUNCTIONAL AREA

EVENT	DESCRIPTION	PAGE
C2OP-IM-2001	Conduct Information Management Planning (IMP)	4-6
C2OP-IM-2002	Execute Information Management Plan	4-7
C2OP-IM-2003	Conduct Information Management Continuing action	4-7
C2OP-INST-2001	Install C2 Software	4-8
C2OP-LOG-2001	Operate Battle Command Support Sustainment System (BCS3)	4-9
C2OP-LOG-2002	Operate Common Logistics Command and Control System (CLC2S)	4-10
C2OP-LOG-2003	Operate Transportation Capacity Planning Tool (TCPT)	4-11
C2OP-LOG-2004	Manage Transportation Capacity Planning Tools (TCPT) Unit and System Network Functions	4-11
C2OP-MAIN-2001	Maintain C2 Systems	4-12
C2OP-MAIN-2002	Protect C2 Systems	4-12
C2OP-MAIN-2003	Maintain the FBCB2 Blue Force Tracking (BFT) equipment	4-13
C2OP-OPER-2001	Operate Command and Control Personal Computer (C2PC)/ Joint Tactical Command Workstation (JTCW) Client	4-14
C2OP-OPER-2002	Operate Command Post of the Future (CPoF)	4-15
C2OP-OPER-2003	Operate FBCB2 Blue Force Tracking (BFT) equipment	4-16
C2OP-OPER-2004	Operate Advanced Field Artillery Tactical Data System (AFATDS)	4-17
C2OP-OPER-2005	Operate Biometric Automated Toolset (BAT) equipment	4-18
C2OP-OPER-2006	Operate Joint Automated Deep Operations Coordination System (JADOCS)	4-19
C2OP-OPER-2007	Operate the Effects Management Tool (EMT)	4-19
C2OP-OPER-2008	Operate SharePoint as a Document Library Manager	4-20
C2OP-OPER-2009	Operate SharePoint as a Basic Site Manager	4-21
C2OP-OPER-2010	Operate an Intelligence Operations Server Version 1 (IOSV1)	4-21
C2OP-OPER-2011	Operate Theater Battle Management Core System (TBMCS)	4-22
C2OP-OPER-2012	Operate the Force Status and Monitoring (FSTAT) Application	4-23
C2OP-OPER-2013	Operate the Execution Status and Monitoring (ESTAT) Application	4-24
C2OP-OPER-2014	Operate the Web Air Request Processor (WARP)	4-25
C2OP-COC-2101	Perform as a COC Watch Officer (WO)	4-25
C2OP-COC-2102	Perform as a COC Watch Chief	4-26
C2OP-COC-2103	Perform as a Journal Clerk	4-27
C2OP-COC-2104	Perform as a Logistic Representative	4-28
C2OP-COC-2105	Perform as an Intelligence Clerk	4-29
C2OP-COC-2106	Perform as a Artillery Liaison Officer	4-29
C2OP-COC-2107	Perform as an Operations Chief within the Operations Center	4-30
C2OP-COC-2108	Perform as a Fire Support Coordinator	4-31
C2OP-COC-2109	Perform as a Communications Watch	4-31
C2OP-COC-2110	Perform as a Air Officer	4-32
C2OP-LOG-2101	Operate Transportation Capacity Planning Tool (TCPT) as Mission Resource Manager	4-33

4003. 2000-LEVEL EVENTS

C2OP-IM-2001: Conduct Information Management Planning (IMP)

EVALUATION-CODED: NO   **SUSTAINMENT INTERVAL**: 12 months

DESCRIPTION: Information Management is the collection and management of information from one or more sources and the distribution of that information to one or more audiences. IM enables commanders and staff to better formulate and analyze COA's, make decisions and execute those decisions in a timely manner.

GRADES: GYSGT, MSGT, MGYSGT, 1STLT, CAPT, MAJ, LTCOL

INITIAL TRAINING SETTING: FORMAL

CONDITION: Given an operations order from higher, planning documents, commander's guidance and references.

STANDARD: To collect, manage and distribute information to satisfy unit's information management requirements.

PERFORMANCE STEPS:
1. Analyze mission.
2. Develop information exchange requirements.
3. Identify unit TO&E C2 systems/collaborative tools.
4. Design architecture for GOTS/COTS C2 systems/collaborative tools.
5. Communicate unit TO&E C2 systems/collaborative tools requirements.
6. Develop the C2 estimate of supportability.
7. Coordinate the C2 estimate of supportability with HAS and cognizant staff.
8. Draft the C2 concept of employment.
9. Draft the purpose of C2 systems/collaborative tools (Mission Specific).
10. Draft the C2 systems' configurations required to establish a common operational picture (COP).
11. Draft configuration management plan for each warfighting functions C2 Systems/collaborative tools.
12. Coordinate with the G6/S6 to ensure the Annex K supports the Annex U.
13. Draft the plan for the information management board (IMP) and information management working group (IMWG).
14. Draft the information management matrix.
15. Draft the joint and coalition C2 interoperability requirements for the execution of C2 in shared battlespace.
16. Give transition brief for information management plan to the commander.
17. Modify information management plan based on commander's guidance.
18. Publish/disseminate the Annex U to MAGTF and MAGTF Subordinate Commands/elements.
19. Refine IM Plan in response to a dynamic operating environment (RIP/TOA, Retrograde, and Redeployment).

REFERENCES:
1. DCOCSOP Digital COC SOP for Battalion Operations in Irregular Warfare
2. MCO 3500.26A Universal Naval Task List (UNTL) Version 3.0 (Jan 07)
3. MCO 3500.27_ Operational Risk Management (ORM)

C2OP-IM-2002: Execute Information Management Plan

EVALUATION-CODED: NO   **SUSTAINMENT INTERVAL**: 12 months

DESCRIPTION: Information Management is the collection and management of information from one or more sources and the distribution of that information to one or more audiences. IM enables commanders and staff to better formulate and analyze COA's, make decisions and execute those decisions in a timely manner.

GRADES: MSGT, MGYSGT, 1STLT, CAPT, MAJ, LTCOL

INITIAL TRAINING SETTING: FORMAL

CONDITION: Given a functional communications network, C2 systems, operations order, commander's guidance and references.

STANDARD: To collect, manage and distribute information to satisfy the commands information management requirements.

PERFORMANCE STEPS:
1. Execute the Annex U2.
2. Implement the commander and staffs information exchange requirements (i.e. doctrinal TTPs (CCIR, PIR, EEFI, FFIR)).
3. Coordinate the implementation of unit TO&E C2 systems/collaborative tools.
4. Implement the new GOTS/COTS C2 systems/collaborative tools architecture specific to new operating environment.
5. Communicate unit TO&E C2 systems/collaborative tools requirements specific to the new operating environment and to supporting establishment.
6. Execute the configurations required to establish a COP.
7. Support the execution of the information management matrix.
8. Coordinate joint and coalition C2 interoperability requirements.

REFERENCES:
1. DCOCSOP Digital COC SOP for Battalion Operations in Irregular Warfare
2. MCDP 6 Command and Control
3. MCDP-5 Planning
4. MCWP 5-1 Marine Corps Planning Process (MCPP)

C2OP-IM-2003: Conduct Information Management (IM) Continuing action

EVALUATION-CODED: NO   **SUSTAINMENT INTERVAL**: 12 months

DESCRIPTION: Information Management is the collection and management of information from one or more sources and the distribution of that information to one or more audiences. IM enables commanders and staff to better formulate and analyze COA's, make decisions and execute those decisions in a timely manner.

GRADES: MSGT, MGYSGT, 1STLT, CAPT, MAJ, LTCOL

INITIAL TRAINING SETTING: FORMAL

CONDITION: Given a functional communications network, C2 systems, operations order, commander's guidance and references.

STANDARD: To collect, manage and distribute information to satisfy the commands information management requirements.

PERFORMANCE STEPS:
1. Conduct information management.
2. Coordinate requirements for the employment and echeloning of C2 capabilities.
3. Maintain the commander and staffs information exchange requirements.
4. Monitor the unit TO&E, and new C2 systems/collaborative tools within the context of operational conditions.
5. Operate C2 systems/collaborative tools.
6. Maintain C2 systems/collaborative tools.
7. Maintain control of the COP configuration.
8. Maintain control of the configuration for each warfighting functions C2 Systems/collaborative tools.
9. Communicate unit TO&E C2 systems/collaborative tools requirements specific to new operating environment and mission to supporting establishment for equipping and training.
10. Chair the IMWG.
11. Report status/results of the IMWG to the IM board.
12. Support the execution of the information management matrix.
13. Coordinate joint and coalition C2 interoperability requirements.
14. Modify the Annex U. (as required)
15. Publish/disseminate Annex U.
16. Refine IM Plan for branches and sequels.

REFERENCES:
1. DCOCSOP Digital COC SOP for Battalion Operations in Irregular Warfare
2. MCDP 6 Command and Control
3. MCDP-5 Planning
4. MCWP 5-1 Marine Corps Planning Process (MCPP)

C2OP-INST-2001: Install C2 Software

EVALUATION-CODED: NO   SUSTAINMENT INTERVAL: 12 months

DESCRIPTION: The proper installation of C2 software is vital to the functioning and integration of C2 systems within the COC.

GRADES: PVT, PFC, LCPL, CPL, SGT, SSGT, GYSGT, MSGT, 2NDLT, 1STLT, CAPT, MAJ

INITIAL TRAINING SETTING: FORMAL

CONDITION: Given C2 systems.

STANDARD: So the software is functional.

PERFORMANCE STEPS:
1. Identify C2 equipment components.
2. Install C2 components.

3. Install C2 software.
4. Configure C2 operating system.

REFERENCES:
1. DCOCSOP Digital COC SOP for Battalion Operations in Irregular Warfare
2. Manufacturer's Technical Instructions and Publications

MISCELLANEOUS:

ADMINISTRATIVE INSTRUCTIONS: The Network Plus course is required before becoming an Administrator for C2 System/Network. Managers/Supervisors would need Security Plus Course designation prior to being assigned.

C2OP-LOG-2001: Operate Battle Command Support Sustainment System (BCS3)

EVALUATION-CODED: NO   SUSTAINMENT INTERVAL: 12 months

DESCRIPTION: Battle Command Sustainment Support System (BCS3) is a C2 System used to track and graphically display logistical support and in-transit visibility (ITV) during all phases of MAGTF operations. The primary users of BCS3 are logistics representatives derived from any of the six functions of Combat Service Support.

BILLETS: Embark Representative, Logistics Representative, Supply Representative, Watch Officer/Watch Chief

GRADES: CPL, SGT, SSGT, GYSGT, MSGT, MGYSGT, CWO-2, CWO-3, CWO-4, CWO-5, CAPT, MAJ

INITIAL TRAINING SETTING: FORMAL

CONDITION: Given an operational BCS3 platform and functioning network architecture.

STANDARD: To track logistics operations and graphically display logistical support.

PERFORMANCE STEPS:
1. Initiate start up procedures
2. Configure maps.
3. Create Common Operational Picture (COP) filters.
4. Create Operational (OP) Views
5. Create Callouts.
6. Create Common Operational Picture (COP) overlays.
7. Communicate with other BCS3 Systems.
8. Create proximity reports.
9. Perform repository management.
10. Implement the briefing tool.
11. Create routes.
12. Create incidents.
13. Create queries.
14. Manage the Unit Task Organization (UTO).
15. Manage information using the Logistics Reporting Tool.

REFERENCES:
1. Battle Command and Sustainment Support System (BCS3)
   https://logmod.hqmc.usmc.mil/bridge/bcs3.html
2. FMFM 4-1 Combat Service Support Operations (PCN 13900027300)

C2OP-LOG-2002: Operate Common Logistics Command and Control System (CLC2S)

EVALUATION-CODED: NO   **SUSTAINMENT INTERVAL:** 12 months

DESCRIPTION: The Common Logistics Command and Control System (CLC2S) is a web based application which manages and tracks the status of personnel, supplies and equipment during all phases of MAGTF Operations. CLC2S can be used by all MAGTF Elements from Company Level Operations Centers and higher. The Logistics Representatives are derived from any of the six functions of Combat Service Support.

BILLETS: Logistics Representative, Supply Representative, Watch Officer/Watch Chief

GRADES: PVT, PFC, LCPL, CPL, SGT, SSGT, GYSGT, MSGT, MGYSGT, WO-1, CWO-2, CWO-3, CWO-4, CWO-5, 2NDLT, 1STLT, CAPT, MAJ

INITIAL TRAINING SETTING: FORMAL

CONDITION: Given a functional communications network, a CLC2S user account and connection to a CLC2S server.

STANDARD: In order to manage and track the status of personnel, supplies and equipment.

PERFORMANCE STEPS:
1. Access CLC2S Server.
2. Create a rapid request in the Rapid Request Tracking System (RRTS+) module.
3. Monitor a rapid request within the RRTS+ Module.
4. Process a rapid request within the RRTS+ Module.
5. Employ the Enhanced CSSOC/COC System (ECS) module.
6. Employ the Logistics Planning and Execution (Log P/E) module.
7. Establish integration with a functioning C2PC Workstation.

REFERENCES:
1. MCO 4105.4 Ground Weapon Systems/Equipment (WS/E) and Automated Information Systems (AIS) Life Cycle Logistics Support
2. MCO P4400.150_ Consumer Level Supply Policy Manual
3. MCO P4790.2_ MIMMS Field Procedures Manual

C2OP-LOG-2003: Operate Transportation Capacity Planning Tool (TCPT)

EVALUATION-CODED: NO   **SUSTAINMENT INTERVAL:** 12 months

DESCRIPTION: Transportation Capacity Planning Tool (TCPT) allows MAGTF Transportation Planners to view transportation capacity in an online environment through an integrated association of Transportation Movement Request (TMR) and personnel and equipment resources, while providing decision makers with a common operational environment and real-time visibility of resources to enable faster reactions to a dynamic wartime environment.

BILLETS: Commodity Manager, Logistics Representative

GRADES: PVT, PFC, LCPL, CPL, SGT, SSGT, GYSGT, MSGT, MGYSGT, WO-1, CWO-2, CWO-3, CWO-4, CWO-5, 2NDLT, 1STLT, CAPT, MAJ

INITIAL TRAINING SETTING: FORMAL

CONDITION: Given a functional communications network, a TCPT user account and connection to a TCPT server.

STANDARD: To coordinate movement and lift requirements.

PERFORMANCE STEPS:
1. Access TCPT.
2. Establish TCPT User Permission.
3. Apply the functions of the Dashboard.
4. Apply the Personnel functions.
5. Apply the Equipment functions.
6. Apply the Transportation functions.
7. Apply the Mission Tracker functions.
8. Execute a Ground Transportation Request.

REFERENCES:
1. MCO P4600.7C USMC Transportation Manual
2. TM 11240-15/3F Motor Vehicle Licensing Official's Manual
3. TM 4700-15/1_ Ground Equipment Record Procedures

C2OP-LOG-2004: Manage Transportation Capacity Planning Tools (TCPT) Unit and System Network Functions

EVALUATION-CODED: NO   **SUSTAINMENT INTERVAL**: 12 months

DESCRIPTION: Transportation Capacity Planning Tool (TCPT) allows MAGTF Transportation Planners to view transportation capacity in an online environment through a integrated association of Transportation Movement Request (TMR) and personnel and equipment resources, while providing decision makers with a common operational environment and real-time visibility of resources to enable faster reactions to a dynamic wartime environment.

BILLETS: Commodity Manager, Logistics Representative

GRADES: CPL, SGT, SSGT, GYSGT, MSGT, MGYSGT, WO-1, CWO-2, CWO-3, CWO-4, 2NDLT, 1STLT, CAPT

INITIAL TRAINING SETTING: FORMAL

CONDITION: Given a functional TCP/IP network, a TCPT user account and connection to a TCPT server and permissions.

STANDARD: To plan and resource unit movement and lift requirements.

PERFORMANCE STEPS:
1. Establish TCPT User Permissions.
2. Execute unit administration functions.
3. Execute system administration functions.

REFERENCES:
1. MCO P4600.7C USMC Transportation Manual
2. TM 11240-15/3F Motor Vehicle Licensing Official's Manual
3. TM 4700-15/1_ Ground Equipment Record Procedures
4. Manufacturer's Technical Instructions and Publications

C2OP-MAIN-2001: Maintain C2 Systems

EVALUATION-CODED: NO   **SUSTAINMENT INTERVAL**: 12 months

DESCRIPTION: Operators and Administrators must be familiar with maintaining the C2 systems within the COC.

GRADES: PVT, PFC, LCPL, CPL, SGT, SSGT, GYSGT, MSGT, 2NDLT, 1STLT, CAPT, LTCOL

INITIAL TRAINING SETTING: FORMAL

CONDITION: Given C2 systems.

STANDARD: So that systems and components are functional.

PERFORMANCE STEPS:
1. Conduct upgrades.
2. Reconfigure C2 infrastructure.
3. Monitor C2 components.
4. Optimize network component performance.
5. Conduct backup.
6. Conduct restore.
7. Repair/Replace defective components.

REFERENCES:
1. Manufacturer's Technical Instructions and Publications

C2OP-MAIN-2002: Protect C2 Systems

EVALUATION-CODED: NO   **SUSTAINMENT INTERVAL**: 12 months

DESCRIPTION: Protection of all C2 Systems and components is vital to maintaining operability and the flow of information and communication within the COC.

GRADES: PVT, PFC, LCPL, CPL, SGT, SSGT, GYSGT, MSGT, 2NDLT, 1STLT, CAPT, MAJ

INITIAL TRAINING SETTING: FORMAL

CONDITION: Given C2 systems.

STANDARD: So that systems and components are available.

PERFORMANCE STEPS:
1. Implement/Develop C2 Systems protection plan.
2. Maintain C2 Systems protection plan.
3. Maintain Physical security of C2 system components and equipment.

REFERENCES:
1. Manufacturer's Technical Instructions and Publications

C2OP-MAIN-2003: Maintain the FBCB2 Blue Force Tracking (BFT) equipment

EVALUATION-CODED: NO   SUSTAINMENT INTERVAL: 12 months

DESCRIPTION: BFT is a battle command information system designed for units performing missions at the tactical level. FBCB2-BFT displays the relevant Situational Awareness (SA) picture of the battlefield. Due to battlefield conditions and utilization of the system the FBCB2 BFT equipment may fail requiring organizational level maintenance to return equipment to an operational state.

GRADES: PVT, PFC, LCPL, CPL, SGT, SSGT, GYSGT, MSGT, 2NDLT, 1STLT, CAPT, MAJ

INITIAL TRAINING SETTING: FORMAL

CONDITION: Given an FBCB2 BFT system with faults.

STANDARD: Perform corrective maintenance steps at the organizational level to return the system to a state of operational readiness.

PERFORMANCE STEPS:
1. Apply Safety procedures.
2. Identify system components
3. Identify system faults.
4. Implement troubleshooting techniques.
5. Troubleshoot malfunctioning components.
6. Replace Parts.
7. Restore system software.
8. Navigate System Administration Menu.
9. Apply the functions of Transceiver Management Tools.
10. Restore system to operational state.
11. Apply the function of Mission Data Loader.
12. Maintain current map data sets.

REFERENCES:
1. TB 11-7010-326-10 BFT FBCB2 Operator's Pocket Guide (Draft) 17 February 2004 - outdated

2. TB 11-7010-326-10-3 TECHNICAL BULLETIN FBCB2/BFT OPERATOR'S POCKET GUIDE For Force XXI Battle Command Brigade-and-Below Blue Force Tracking (FBCB2/BFT) Computer Set, Digital AN/UYK-128(V)
3. TM 11180A-OI/4 TECHNICAL MANUAL/OPERATOR AND FIELD MAINTENANCE MANUAL INCLUDING REPAIR PARTS AND SPECIAL TOOLS LIST FORFORCE XXI BATTLE COMMAND BRIGADE-AND-BELOW (FBCB2)-BLUEFORCE TRACKING (BFT) TACTICAL OPERATIONS CENTER (TOC) SYSTEM
4. TM 1I180A-OR TECHNICAL MANUAL/OPERATORS MANUAL FORFORCE XXI BATTLE COMMAND BRIGADE-AND-BELOW (FBCB2)-BLUE FORCE TRACKING COMPUTER SET, DIGITALAN/UYK-128(V) AN/UYK-128(V)1(NSN: 7010-01-475-5277) (EIC:K2S)AN/UYK-128(V)3 (NSN: 7010-01-513-8459) (EIC:K2U) DISTRIBUTION
5. TM 11180A-OR   Technical Manual Operator's Manual for Force XXI Battle Command Brigade-and-Below (FBCB2)-Blue Force Tracking (BFT) Computer Set, Digital AN/UYK-128(V) AN/UYK-128(V)1 (NSN: 7010-01-475-5277) (EIC:K2S) AN/UYK-128(V)3 (NSN: 7010-01-513-8459) (EIC:K2U)

C2OP-OPER-2001: Operate Command and Control Personal Computer (C2PC)/ Joint Tactical Command Workstation (JTCW) Client

EVALUATION-CODED: NO   **SUSTAINMENT INTERVAL:** 12 months

DESCRIPTION: Intelligence Operations Workstation (IOW) is the equipment suite, which provides automated support to the COC via the C2 application called C2PC/ JTCW Client. An IOW is simply a laptop inside the COC, which is pre-loaded with C2PC or JTCW Client and many other software applications. C2PC/JTCW Client provides map overlays, friendly unit locations with status and plans of intended movement, and hostile unit locations. C2PC/ JTCW Client is linked together within the COC via a Local Area Network (LAN) allowing rapid information exchange between staff sections, and they are also linked with adjacent, subordinate, and higher headquarters via a Wide Area Network (WAN). C2PC/JTCW Client provides an automated message generation and validation capability for the exchange of MTF messages and a capability to generate and validate Variable Message Format (VMF) messages. C2PC/JTCW Client has multiple application extensions that allow modular systems with an interface with other capabilities such as AFATDS through the Effects Management Tool (EMT) and Blue Force Tracker (BFT).

GRADES: PVT, PFC, LCPL, CPL, SGT, SSGT, GYSGT, MSGT, MGYSGT, WO-1, CWO-2, 2NDLT, 1STLT, CAPT, MAJ

INITIAL TRAINING SETTING: FORMAL

CONDITION: Given a computer (IOW) with the current version of JTCW installed, a functional network and Common Tactical Picture (CTP)/Common Operational Picture (COP) architecture.

STANDARD: In order to produce timely and accurate data to satisfy operational requirements.

PERFORMANCE STEPS:
1. Install C2PC/JTCW Client on an IOW
2. Perform a role based log in.
3. Identify features of the C2PC/JTCW Client main window.

4. Apply the toolbar functions of C2PC/JTCW Client toolbars.
5. Apply the functions of the Communication Subsystem.
6. Configure the C2PC/JTCW gateway manager.
7. Configure the C2PC/JTCW Client.
8. Employ mapping products in C2PC/JTCW Client
9. Apply the functions of the Routes Application Extension (AE).
10. Apply the functions of Utilize the Overlays AE.
11. Apply the functions of Utilize the Decision Support Toolbox (DSTB) AE.
12. Manipulate the Track plot AE.
13. Use C2PC/JTCW Client to create MS products (from C2PC/JTCW Client).

RELATED EVENTS: C2OP-OPER-2002

REFERENCES:
1. DCOCSOP Digital COC SOP for Battalion Operations in Irregular Warfare
2. Manufacturer's Technical Instructions and Publications

C2OP-OPER-2002: Operate Command Post of the Future (CPoF)

EVALUATION-CODED: NO   **SUSTAINMENT INTERVAL:** 12 months

DESCRIPTION: CPoF is a C2 software suite hosted on a computer system that provides collaboration and visualization tools to the COC Staff. CPoF is a decision support system that provides situational awareness and collaborative tools to support decision making, planning, rehearsal, and execution management down to the battalion level.

GRADES: PVT, PFC, LCPL, CPL, SGT, SSGT, GYSGT, MSGT, WO-1, CWO-2, 2NDLT, 1STLT, CAPT, MAJ

INITIAL TRAINING SETTING: FORMAL

CONDITION: Given an operational CPoF workstation, a functional CPoF architecture.

STANDARD: In order to share situational awareness and collaborate across the CPoF network.

PERFORMANCE STEPS:
1. Configure the CPOF client terminal.
2. Manage CPoF Map data for the client terminal.
3. Apply the functions of the 2D/CoMotion application.
4. Apply the functions of the 2D/CoMotion Stickies.
5. Apply the functions of the 2D/CoMotion Toolbar.
6. Apply the functions of the 2D/CoMotion Graphics Palette.
7. Apply the functions of the 3D/CommandSight application.
8. Apply the functions of the 3D/CommandSight Graphics Palette.
9. Apply the functions of shared products.
10. Employ tables to manipulate CPoF data.
11. Utilize the Tasks and Schedule feature in CPoF.
12. Integrate data from other C2 Systems.

13. Display images in CPoF. (SNAGIT)
14. Communicate with embedded communications application (VENTRILO).
15. Conduct a Commanders brief.

CHAINED EVENTS: C2OP-OPER-2001

RELATED EVENTS: C2OP-OPER-2001

REFERENCES:
1. CPOF - Command Sight Users Manual V3.0 Command Sight reference manual
2. CPOF - MAPMAN 3.1.0.0 Administrators Guide Document Ver 1.1
3. CPOF TB-11-7010-409-13 ver 3.0.2 P2 Command Post of the Future (CPOF)
4. CPOF TB-11-7010-464-13 ver QR-1 Command Post of the Future QR-1 (latest version)
5. DCOCSOP Digital COC SOP for Battalion Operations in Irregular Warfare

---

C2OP-OPER-2003: Operate FBCB2 Blue Force Tracking (BFT) equipment

EVALUATION-CODED: NO   **SUSTAINMENT INTERVAL**: 12 months

DESCRIPTION: BFT is a battle command information system designed for units performing missions at the tactical level. FBCB2-BFT displays the relevant Situational Awareness (SA) picture of the battlefield. BFT displays location of the user, other friendly forces, observed enemy locations, and all known battlefield obstacles. Additionally, BFT allows users to communicate. BFT is employed by the battalion COC, company COC, convoys and/or patrols traversing throughout the battalion area of operations.

GRADES: PVT, PFC, LCPL, CPL, SGT, SSGT, GYSGT, MSGT, WO-1, CWO-2, 2NDLT, 1STLT, CAPT, MAJ

INITIAL TRAINING SETTING: FORMAL

CONDITION: Given a functional FBCB2 BFT system with functional network.

STANDARD: So that all performance steps are completed in support of the units mission.

PERFORMANCE STEPS:
1. Prepare FBCB2 BFT for use.
2. Configure system for use.
3. Manage map views.
4. Manage user folders.
5. Manage messages.
6. Process messages.
7. Process overlays.
8. Manage filters.
9. Create navigation route.
10. Apply the functions of the application tools.
11. Employ security features.
12. Secure BFT system.

REFERENCES:
1. DCOCSOP Digital COC SOP for Battalion Operations in Irregular Warfare
2. Manufacturer's Operating Instructions
3. Manufacturer's Technical Instructions and Publications

C2OP-OPER-2004: Operate Advanced Field Artillery Tactical Data System (AFATDS)

EVALUATION-CODED: NO   **SUSTAINMENT INTERVAL:** 12 months

DESCRIPTION: AFATDS provides an automated capability for fire planning, tactical fire direction, and fire support coordination at the firing battery, fire direction center (FDC), and fire support coordination center (FSCC). AFATDS assists the commander in improving tactical planning and control of supporting arms operations. AFATDS provides an automated capability to integrate supporting arms assets into maneuver plans, provide battlefield information, target analysis, and unit status, while coordinating target damage assessment and sensor operations. The AFATDS workstation receives, transmits, edits, displays and processes fire support requests and stores data to facilitate artillery fire support direction and coordination. A full range of fire support, maneuver control, coordination measures, and geometry are displayed for support coordination at the workstation. AFATDS operates within the existing and planned communication architecture and assists the commander with automated message delivery for coordination of supporting arms fires.

GRADES: LCPL, CPL, SGT, SSGT, GYSGT, WO-1, CWO-2, CWO-3, 2NDLT, 1STLT, CAPT, MAJ

INITIAL TRAINING SETTING: FORMAL

CONDITION: Given a functional AFATDS workstation and a functional network.

STANDARD: To provide timely and accurate fire support.

PERFORMANCE STEPS:
1. Load AFATDS.
2. Initialize AFATDS.
3. Activate the workstation.
4. Display the "Current Situation".
5. Build a planned communications configuration.
6. Edit the database.
7. Conduct Mission Processing.
8. Conduct Fire Planning.
9. Troubleshoot AFATDS.
10. Perform proper shut down procedures.

REFERENCES:
1. DCOCSOP Digital COC SOP for Battalion Operations in Irregular Warfare
2. MCWP 3-16 Fire Support Coordination in the Ground Combat Element
3. TB 11-7025-297-10 AFATDS Operators Notebook
4. TM 11-7025-279-10-1 AFATDS Users Manual

C2OP-OPER-2005: Operate Biometric Automated Toolset (BAT) equipment

EVALUATION-CODED: NO   **SUSTAINMENT INTERVAL**: 12 months

DESCRIPTION: BAT provides a means of identifying individuals via fingerprints, iris scan, and photo identification (ID) which enables the creation of individual records. The system includes a laptop with the BAT software, a fingerprint scanner, an iris scanner, a digital camera, and an ID card printer. ID badges can be provided to residents of a city or other identified geographic area. Local residents can be easily identified by friendly forces at entry control points with the use of identification badges. The Marine can access an individual's information such birth date, occupation, place of residence, and any documentation addressing affiliation with anyone involved in terrorist activities. Although BAT may not reside directly in the Bn COC, all COC staff members must be aware of its capabilities.

GRADES: PVT, PFC, LCPL, CPL, SGT, SSGT, GYSGT, WO-1, CWO-2, 2NDLT, 1STLT, CAPT, MAJ

INITIAL TRAINING SETTING: FORMAL

CONDITION: Given functional BAT equipment and associated peripherals.

STANDARD: In order to support the established force protection measures within an AO.

PERFORMANCE STEPS:
1. Connect peripherals to BAT Client.
2. Activate peripherals.
3. Troubleshoot peripherals.
4. Initialize BAT Client.
5. Perform identification.
6. Interpret color codes for personal data identification.
7. Understand person and entity searches/queries.
8. Collect Biometrics.
9. Enter an individual's information into the BAT system.
10. Create badges (resident/non-resident).
11. Review dossiers.
12. Manage reports.
13. Capture iris with Piers 2.4 untethered from BAT client
14. Upload/download images from BAT client.
15. Demonstrate file transfer from BAT server to client.

REFERENCES:
1. BAT IAW Biometric Automated Tool Set User Guide
2. DCOCSOP Digital COC SOP for Battalion Operations in Irregular Warfare

---

C2OP-OPER-2006: Operate Joint Automated Deep Operations Coordination System (JADOCS)

EVALUATION-CODED: NO   **SUSTAINMENT INTERVAL**: 12 months

DESCRIPTION: The Joint Automated Deep Operations Coordination System
(JADOCS) provides the warfighter with a timely, accurate, detailed
battlespace view for planning, coordination, and execution of targets. It is
a joint mission management software application that provides a suite of
tools and interfaces for horizontal and vertical integration across
battlespace functional areas.

GRADES: PVT, PFC, LCPL, CPL, SGT, SSGT, GYSGT, WO-1, CWO-2, 2NDLT, 1STLT,
CAPT, MAJ

INITIAL TRAINING SETTING: FORMAL

CONDITION: Given a functional JADOCS system and functional communications
architecture.

STANDARD: In order to provide a timely, accurate and detailed battlespace
view for planning and collaboration of fires.

PERFORMANCE STEPS:
1. Manipulate user preferences within JADOCS
2. Configure JADOCS View Options.
3. Manage JADOCS Overlays.
4. Apply the functions of Tools within JADOCS.
5. Employ Map functions.
6. Communicate using Chat function.
7. Manage databases.
8. Identify JADOCS Managers.
9. Monitor Mission Status.
10. Manage Target Data Card.
11. Apply the functions of the Artillery Manager.
12. Apply the functions of Air Support Manager.
13. Display engagement zones.
14. Manipulate Counter fire COP.
15. Transmit TGT.
16. Employ ATO Manager.
17. Track Close Air Support Missions.

RELATED EVENTS:
C2OP-OPER-2004   C2OP-OPER-2001

REFERENCES:
1. DCOCSOP Digital COC SOP for Battalion Operations in Irregular Warfare
2. JADOCS ver 1.0.3.5 Build 25 Mar 2008 Joint Automated Deep Operations
    Coordination System

C2OP-OPER-2007: Operate the Effects Management Tool (EMT)

EVALUATION-CODED: NO   **SUSTAINMENT INTERVAL**: 12 months

DESCRIPTION: EMT provides an injector for C2PC, which provides track data
enabling increased situational awareness to the commander and his staff.

GRADES: PVT, PFC, LCPL, CPL, SGT, SSGT, GYSGT, WO-1, CWO-2, CWO-3, 2NDLT, 1STLT, CAPT, MAJ

INITIAL TRAINING SETTING: FORMAL

CONDITION: Given a computer loaded with the current version of C2PC/JTCW with AFATDS compatible version of EMT, a functional network and Common Tactical Picture (CTP) architecture, an operational AFATDS machine.

STANDARD: So that all performance steps are completed in support of the units mission.

PERFORMANCE STEPS:
1. Configure EMT version for use. (Uninstall and load).
2. Create EMT user within AFATDS.
3. Establish a connection.
4. Apply the functions of the main menu bar.
5. Manage maps.
6. Locate C2PC overlays.
7. Set up user preferences.
8. Load map products. (DTED, CADRG).
9. Filter unit data.
10. Report change in unit location.
11. View unit task organization.
12. Create geometry.
13. Edit geometry.
14. Export/Import geometry worksheet to excel spread sheet.
15. Create a target.
16. Import /Export target worksheet.
17. Initiate a fire mission.
18. Create the Air Support List (ASL).
19. Create an air nomination.
20. Update ASL.

RELATED EVENTS: C2OP-OPER-2004

REFERENCES:
1. DCOCSOP Digital COC SOP for Battalion Operations in Irregular Warfare
2. Manufacturer's Technical Instructions and Publications

C2OP-OPER-2008: Operate SharePoint as a Document Library Manager

EVALUATION-CODED: NO   SUSTAINMENT INTERVAL: 12 months

DESCRIPTION: SharePoint is a web based collaborative tool. All operational and garrison billets can manipulate regularly viewed documents/information while allowing multiple users simultaneous access in place of the share drive. Document Library Manager can organize and display information pertinent to the mission.

GRADES: PVT, PFC, LCPL, CPL, SGT, SSGT, GYSGT, 1STSGT, MSGT, MGYSGT, WO-1, CWO-2, CWO-3, CWO-5, 2NDLT, 1STLT, CAPT, MAJ, LTCOL

INITIAL TRAINING SETTING: FORMAL

CONDITION: Given a SharePoint site with appropriate permissions and a functional communications network.

STANDARD: To organize and display information pertinent commands information management requirements.

PERFORMANCE STEPS:
1. Navigate site.
2. Manage document libraries.
3. Manage web parts.
4. Manage recycle bin.

C2OP-OPER-2009: Operate SharePoint as a Basic Site Manager

EVALUATION-CODED: NO   **SUSTAINMENT INTERVAL**: 12 months

DESCRIPTION: All operational and garrison billets can organize lists and libraries in a web based collaborative environment to optimize Information Management.

GRADES: PVT, PFC, LCPL, CPL, SGT, SSGT, GYSGT, 1STSGT, MSGT, MGYSGT, WO-1, CWO-2, CWO-3, CWO-4, CWO-5, 2NDLT, 1STLT, CAPT, MAJ, LTCOL

INITIAL TRAINING SETTING: FORMAL

CONDITION: Given a SharePoint site with appropriate permissions and a functional communications network.

STANDARD: To organize and display information pertinent commands information management requirements.

PERFORMANCE STEPS:
1. Manage document libraries.
2. Manage lists.
3. Manage pictures.
4. Manage web parts.
5. Develop a site structure.
6. Create web part pages/libraries.
7. Establish permissions.

C2OP-OPER-2010: Operate an Intelligence Operations Server Version 1 (IOSV1)

EVALUATION-CODED: NO   **SUSTAINMENT INTERVAL**: 12 months

DESCRIPTION: The Intelligence Operations Server Version 1 (IOSV1) is a fully self contained server that uses a UNIX based Sun Solaris operating system. IOSV1 facilitates dissemination of command and control information between adjacent, higher, and subordinate commands via a Wide Area Network (WAN). The IOSV1 is primarily located at regiment and higher echelon units, where the Common Operational Picture (COP) is stored, maintained, and distributed. Chat capabilities are established utilizing the IOSV1 as a server which provides the capability for units to establish communication with each other. The IOSV1 most commonly works in conjunction with Command and Control Personal Computer (C2PC) for COP Management. In addition, Blue Force Tracker (BFT) communicates to the IOSV1 via the Global Command and Control System (GCCS) facilitating data sharing between these systems.

GRADES: LCPL, CPL, SGT, SSGT, GYSGT, MSGT, WO-1, CWO-2, 2NDLT, 1STLT

INITIAL TRAINING SETTING: FORMAL

CONDITION: Given an IOS V1 with the current software, a functional network, network topology, and Common Tactical Picture (CTP)/Common Operational Picture (COP) architecture.

STANDARD: In order to maintain stable network communications ensuring Command and Control (C2) tactical information flow in support of unit operations.

PERFORMANCE STEPS:
1. Install current software
2. Input basic UNIX commands
3. Operate the DII COE menu
4. Manage the root account
5. Manage the SYSADMIN account
6. Apply the network configuration
7. Configure communication channels
8. Manage the SECMAN account
9. Utilize the Universal Communication Processor (UCP)
10. Manage the USER account
11. Employ the COMMS applications
12. Configure the CST functions
13. Manipulate the Chart window
14. Manipulate message functions
15. Use the segment installer
16. Utilize Go Global
17. Manage IRC application
18. Perform troubleshooting methods
19. Perform Common Operational Picture (COP) management functions

---

C2OP-OPER-2011: Operate Theater Battle Management Core System (TBMCS)

EVALUATION-CODED: NO   **SUSTAINMENT INTERVAL:** 12 months

DESCRIPTION: The Theater Battle Management Core Systems (TBMCS) provides Joint and Service Combat Air Forces with automated Command, Control, Communications, Computer, and Intelligence systems to plan and execute theater-level air campaigns. TBMCS is the theater air module of the Global Command and Control System (GCCS) and includes the Force and Unit Contingency Theater Automated Planning System (CTAPS), Combat Intelligence System (CIS), Wing Command and Control System (WCCS), and the Air Support Operations Center (ASOC) top-level applications. Elements of TBMCS are planned for every theater air command and control and air weapons system from the Joint Forces Air Component Commander to the executing aircraft squadron. The mission of TBMCS at the force level is to provide the Joint and Combined Air Component Commander with the automated tools necessary to effectively and efficiently plan, monitor, and execute the air campaign. This includes planning and issuing the Air Tasking and Air Control Orders that ensure the Theater Commander's intent is supported through the application of airpower using the latest intelligence. TBMCS capabilities should also ensure that air operations are de-conflicted. The mission of TBMCS at the unit level is to provide the Wing and Base Commanders and their battle staffs with timely and accurate information for effective decision making. TBMCS is also supposed to provide the secure, automated, deployable, and distributed Wing-Level Command and Control System with connectivity to force-level TBMCS systems

GRADES: PFC, LCPL, CPL, SGT, SSGT, GYSGT, MSGT, MGYSGT, WO-1, CWO-2, CWO-3, CWO-4, CWO-5, 1STLT, CAPT, MAJ

INITIAL TRAINING SETTING: FORMAL

CONDITION: Given an operational SIPR networked TBMCS Client workstation and appropriate TBMCS user permissions

STANDARD: To provide the Commanders and their battle staffs with timely and accurate information for effective decision making.

PERFORMANCE STEPS:
1. Access CAOC Central Web (CCWeb).
2. Initiate TBMCS application.
3. Apply the functions of the Web Air Request Processor (WARP).
4. Apply the functions of the Execution Status and Monitoring (ESTAT) tool.
5. Apply the functions of the Force Status and Monitoring (FSTAT) tool.

C2OP-OPER-2012: Operate the Force Status and Monitoring (FSTAT) Application

EVALUATION-CODED: NO   **SUSTAINMENT INTERVAL**: 12 months

DESCRIPTION: FSTAT allows the user to report and modify FrOB status using six products: ADA Unit Status, Aircraft Unit Status, Base Status, Surface C2 Unit Status, Missile Unit Status and Fire Unit Status. These products provide queuing of data updates enabling the user to operate through intermittent communication outages. They provide links into the OPAGEs that provide more data on the selected item.

INITIAL TRAINING SETTING: FORMAL

CONDITION: Given an operational SIPR networked functional PC (TBMCS Client) workstation, desk top procedures/SOP and appropriate TBMCS user permissions.

STANDARD: to monitor and update the Aviation Friendly Order of Battle Status

PERFORMANCE STEPS:
1. Select appropriate force status.
2. Create user defined filters.

3. Set GUI customized settings.
4. Establish user defined views.
5. Export reports.
6. Plot current information to Map Product.

REFERENCES:
1. Manufacturer's Technical Instructions and Publications

C2OP-OPER-2013: Operate the Execution Status and Monitoring (ESTAT) Application

EVALUATION-CODED: NO   **SUSTAINMENT INTERVAL:** 12 months

DESCRIPTION: ESTAT allows update and/or review of data on any Air Battle Plan (ABP) in the Air Operations Database (AODB) and allows work in either a tabular or graphical GANTT style display interchangeably. The user can open multiple, independently configurable, filterable, sortable and nameable displays of the retrieved data. Updates made in one display are automatically shown in all ESTAT displays for that retrieved data. ESTAT can be run in an Auto-Update mode that allows the display to reflect the changes made by other clients to the AODB. ESTAT allows the user to plot air and missile routes on the web-based map and provides a link to the Execution Management Map Control Panel (EMMCP) for plotting other relevant operations data such as airspace, targets, bases and unit locations. ESTAT users can update the following mission information: ABP State, Air mission status, Estimated and actual mission event times, Air mission results, Capability to group missions, Number of canceled and/or added aircraft, Actual mission configuration/Standard Configuration Load (SCL), mission deviations, Ground alert response time, Residual mission code. ESTAT users can create, edit and delete Wide Area Geographic (WAG) activities. Use the Execution Status and Monitoring (ESTAT) tool to monitor and update the Air Battle Plan (ABP) in the Air Operations Database (AODB).

INITIAL TRAINING SETTING: FORMAL

CONDITION: Given an operational SIPR networked functional PC (TBMCS Client) workstation, desk top procedures/SOP and appropriate TBMCS user permissions.

STANDARD: to monitor and update the Air Battle Plan (ABP) in the Air Operations Database (AODB) to provide the Commanders and their battle staffs with timely and accurate information for effective decision making.

PERFORMANCE STEPS:
1. Establish user defined views.
2. Establish user defined filters.
3. Plot routes (air/missles).
4. Plot operations data (airspace, targets, bases and units).
5. Update the selected ABP.
6. Update mission information.
7. Manage Mission Deviations.
8. Manage Wide Area Geographic (WAG) Activities.

C2OP-OPER-2014: Operate the Web Air Request Processor (WARP)

EVALUATION-CODED: NO   **SUSTAINMENT INTERVAL:** 12 months

DESCRIPTION: The WARP application interfaces between a web browser and the Air Operations Database (AODB). The user interface to WARP is generated from Hyper Text Markup Language (HTML), viewable with a web browser. The user can submit, view, and edit Joint Tactical Air Strike Requests/Joint Tactical Air Requests (JTASRs/JTARs) and Assault Support Requests (ASRs) using WARP. The user can view and send Tactical Air Control Party (TACP) Free Text messages, as well as view TACP Status messages. The user can also assign missions to requests and issue scramble orders from WARP. The WARP application interfaces with various maps through the MAPAPI and Map Manager (MAPMGR) segments. JTASRs/JTARs, ASRs, and TACP units can be displayed on a map display. Use the WARP application to submit, view, and edit JTASRs/JTARs and ASRs; view and send TACP Free Text messages; view TACP Status messages; assign missions to requests and issue scramble orders.

INITIAL TRAINING SETTING: FORMAL

CONDITION: Given an operational SIPR networked functional PC (TBMCS Client) workstation, desk top procedures/SOP and appropriate TBMCS user permissions.

STANDARD: To manage preplanned and immediate JTASR/JTARs and ASRs in accordance with priority of fires and scheme of maneuver to support MAGTF operational requirements.

PERFORMANCE STEPS:
1. Initiate WARP.
2. Access the control panel.
3. Create an air request.
4. View summaries
5. Set auto update frequency.
6. View auto update log.
7. Refresh data from Server.
8. Manage requests.
9. Query missions.
10. Submit BDA report.
11. Delete requests.

REFERENCES:
1. Manufacturer's Technical Instructions and Publications

C2OP-COC-2101: Perform as a COC Watch Officer (WO)

EVALUATION-CODED: NO   **SUSTAINMENT INTERVAL:** 12 months

DESCRIPTION: The Watch Officer is the commander's representative and is responsible for the smooth and efficient functioning of the Combat Operations Center (COC) and for the rapid dissemination of information to and from the COC. WO is responsible for coordinating and ensuring proper response to developing events within the COC. In the absence of key leaders the WO is responsible for the execution of the commander's intent and facilitates battle management. The Watch Chief assists the Watch Officer in the performance of his duties.

GRADES: SSGT, GYSGT, MSGT, WO-1, CWO-2, CWO-3, 2NDLT, 1STLT, CAPT, MAJ

INITIAL TRAINING SETTING: FORMAL

CONDITION: Given an operational COC and battle staff, functional communications architecture, current unit TO&E, and C2 systems.

STANDARD: To ensure proper response to developing events.

PERFORMANCE STEPS:
1. Monitor C2 information.
2. Maintain Common Tactical Picture.
3. Maintain overlays.
4. Monitor status boards.
5. Monitor communication systems.
6. Receive information.
7. Analyze information.
8. Prioritize information.
9. Organize information.
10. Distribute information.
11. Record information.
12. Implement decision support tools.
13. Direct the actions of the COC and staff.
14. Conduct battle drills.
15. Coordinate actions with Higher, Adjacent, and Supporting units.
16. Supervise watch standers.
17. Conduct turnover brief.

REFERENCES:
1. DCOCSOP Digital COC SOP for Battalion Operations in Irregular Warfare
2. MCDP 1-0 Marine Corps Operations
3. MCWP 6-2 MAGTF Command and Control Operations
4. MEF C2 Systems Integration Plan Marine Expeditionary Force Command and Control Systems Integration Plan Mar 2006

C2OP-COC-2102: Perform as a COC Watch Chief

EVALUATION-CODED: NO   **SUSTAINMENT INTERVAL**: 12 months

DESCRIPTION: The Watch Chief is responsible for the management of personnel, security and general efficiency of the battle rhythm within the COC. The Watch Chief assists the Watch Officer in the performance of duties as well.

GRADES: SSGT, GYSGT, MSGT, MGYSGT

INITIAL TRAINING SETTING: FORMAL

CONDITION: Given an operational COC and battle staff, functional communications architecture, current unit TO&E, and C2 systems.

STANDARD: To ensure proper response to developing events.

PERFORMANCE STEPS:
1. Control COC access.
2. Monitor C2 information.
3. Maintain Common Tactical Picture.
4. Maintain overlays.
5. Monitor status boards.
6. Monitor communication systems.
7. Receive information.
8. Analyze information.
9. Prioritize information.
10. Organize information.
11. Distribute information.
12. Record information.
13. Implement decision support tools.
14. Direct the actions of the COC and staff. (as required)
15. Conduct battle drills.
16. Coordinate actions with Higher, Adjacent, and Supporting units.
17. Supervise watch standers.
18. Conduct Turnover Brief.

REFERENCES:
1. DCOCSOP Digital COC SOP for Battalion Operations in Irregular Warfare
2. MEF C2 Systems Integration Plan Marine Expeditionary Force Command and Control Systems Integration Plan Mar 2006

C2OP-COC-2103: Perform as a Journal Clerk

EVALUATION-CODED: NO   **SUSTAINMENT INTERVAL:** 12 months

DESCRIPTION: The mission of the journal clerk is to capture, organize, document, and maintain information, message traffic, and significant events (SIGEVENT) activity flowing through the COC. He assists the WO in maintaining digital log books and ensures that any yellow canaries taken by radio operators are converted to digital means using specified collaborative tools.

GRADES: PFC, LCPL, CPL

INITIAL TRAINING SETTING: FORMAL

CONDITION: Given an operational COC, functional communications architecture, current unit TO&E, and C2 systems.

STANDARD: In order to capture, organize, document, and maintain information, message traffic, and significant events (SIGEVENT).

PERFORMANCE STEPS:
1. Receive reports and message traffic.
2. Organize reports and message traffic.
3. Document reports and message traffic.
4. Maintain reports and message traffic.

5. Assist WO/WC. (as required)
6. Monitor assigned collaborative tools. (tactical chat rooms, Portals, Wikis, etc.)
7. Enter certified reports and messages into journal. (certified means approved by WO/WC)
8. Assist with CTP maintenance. (as required)
9. Conduct turnover brief. (as required)

REFERENCES:
1. DCOCSOP Digital COC SOP for Battalion Operations in Irregular Warfare

---

C2OP-COC-2104: Perform as a Logistic Representative

EVALUATION-CODED: NO   **SUSTAINMENT INTERVAL:** 12 months

DESCRIPTION: The S-4 section maintains LOG stats, Unit Movement Control Center (UMCC) boards (in close coordination with the S-3), and performs all other associated S-4 functions. The S-4 section may utilize logistics-specific C2 systems within the COC.

GRADES: SSGT, GYSGT, 1STLT, CAPT

INITIAL TRAINING SETTING: FORMAL

CONDITION: Given an operational COC, functional communications architecture, current unit TO&E, and C2 systems.

STANDARD: In order to maintain LOG stats and Unit Movement Control Center (UMCC) boards.

PERFORMANCE STEPS:
1. Monitor Essential Elements of Friendly Information (EEFIs).
2. Monitor convoy movement control measures.
3. Update TMCC boards.
4. Receive logistics request from subordinate units.
5. Request logistics support from higher.
6. Maintain situational awareness of unit logistics and supply status.
7. Conduct turnover brief. (as required)

REFERENCES:
1. Battle Command and Sustainment Support System (BCS3)
   https://logmod.hqmc.usmc.mil/bridge/bcs3.html
2. DCOCSOP Digital COC SOP for Battalion Operations in Irregular Warfare
3. MCWP 4_1 LOGISTICS OPERATIONS

C2OP-COC-2105: Perform as an Intelligence Clerk

EVALUATION-CODED: NO   **SUSTAINMENT INTERVAL:** 12 months

DESCRIPTION: The Intel representative collects, analyzes, evaluates, and interprets intelligence and continually updates the enemy situation. This information is provided to enhance current and future operations planning. Additionally, they implement and execute the intelligence cycle as directed by the S-2 Officer in support of the battalion's scheme of maneuver. The S-2 section must identify the enemy's most probable and most dangerous COAs, and act as the CTP Manager for enemy tracks created by the battalion and its subordinate units.

GRADES: PFC, LCPL, CPL, SGT

INITIAL TRAINING SETTING: FORMAL

CONDITION: Given an operational COC, functional communications architecture, current unit TO&E, and C2 systems.

STANDARD: In order to implement and execute the intelligence cycle within the COC.

PERFORMANCE STEPS:
1. Monitor current intelligence reports.
2. Report current intelligence status.
3. Report current weather that may impact current operations.
4. Monitor ISR feeds.
5. Conduct turnover brief. (as required)
6. Monitor current significant actions/events (SIGACTS/ SIGEVENTS).
7. Monitor Intel sensors, as appropriate.

REFERENCES:
1. DCOCSOP Digital COC SOP for Battalion Operations in Irregular Warfare
2. MCWP 2-1 Intelligence Operations

C2OP-COC-2106: Perform as a Artillery Liaison Officer

EVALUATION-CODED: NO   **SUSTAINMENT INTERVAL**: 12 months

DESCRIPTION: The Artillery LNO coordinates artillery support with the FSC, S-3, and the commander.

GRADES: 1STLT, CAPT, MAJ

INITIAL TRAINING SETTING: FORMAL

CONDITION: Given an operational COC, functional communications architecture, current unit TO&E, supporting fires, and C2 systems.

STANDARD: To ensure timely process of fires and coordination with maneuver commander's requirements.

PERFORMANCE STEPS:
1. Monitor the artillery conduct of fire (COF) net.
2. Provide clearance on requests for fire.
3. Monitor the artillery battalion and regiment fire direction net.
4. Pass requirements for fire support to the appropriate FDC for action.

5. Maintain situational awareness of current operational status of fire support assets.
6. Maintain situational awareness of logistical status of fire support assets.
7. Keep the FSC informed.
8. Keep the S-2 Representative advised of all target information received through artillery nets.

REFERENCES:
1. DCOCSOP Digital COC SOP for Battalion Operations in Irregular Warfare
2. MCWP 3-16 Fire Support Coordination in the Ground Combat Element

---

C2OP-COC-2107: Perform as an Operations Chief within the Operations Center

EVALUATION-CODED: NO   SUSTAINMENT INTERVAL: 12 months

DESCRIPTION: The Operations Chief is in charge of the establishment and daily functions of the Operations Center. The Ops Chief supervises the updating of the operations maps, operations journal and Common Tactical Picture while ensuring timely, accurate, and complete reports and message routing within the Operations Center. He will publish a Operations Center watch schedule. The operations chief will assist in the preparations of Frag Orders and overlays for dissemination throughout the command.

GRADES: GYSGT, MSGT, MGYSGT

INITIAL TRAINING SETTING: FORMAL

CONDITION: Given an Operations Center (COC, ALOC), functional communications architecture, current unit TO&E, supporting fires, and C2 systems.

STANDARD: To ensure daily operations within the Operations Center is maintained.

PERFORMANCE STEPS:
1. Supervise the establishment/displacement of the Operations Center (COC, ALOC).
2. Supervise the actions of all personnel within the Operations Center (COC, ALOC).
3. Supervise the use of C2 systems/collaborative tools.
4. Supervise the management of classified information.
5. Supervise preparation of the operational journal file.
6. Establish the watch rotation.
7. Assemble operations orders.
8. Distribute operations orders.
9. Supervise the preparation of reports and messages.
10. Supervise the distribution of reports and messages.
11. Supervise the preparation of briefs.
12. Coordinate establishment of Operations Center security with the Camp Commandant.

REFERENCES:
1. DCOCSOP Digital COC SOP for Battalion Operations in Irregular Warfare

---

C2OP-COC-2108: Perform as a Fire Support Coordinator

EVALUATION-CODED: NO   SUSTAINMENT INTERVAL: 12 months

DESCRIPTION: The FSC is responsible for the overall operation, organization, and functioning of the Fire Support Coordination Center (FSCC) within the COC. He translates the concept of fire support into a specific fire support plan and then supervises its execution by the supporting agencies.

GRADES: CAPT, MAJ

INITIAL TRAINING SETTING: MOJT

CONDITION: Given an operational COC and battle staff, functional communications architecture, using current unit T/E, communication assets and relevant C2 systems.

STANDARD: So that all performance steps are completed during COC shift in support of the mission requirements of the unit.

PERFORMANCE STEPS:
1. Supervise the FSCC.
2. Coordinate fire support for the battalion.
3. Monitor fire support and conduct of fire nets.
4. Conduct fire support actions.
5. Maintain situational awareness charts and maps.
6. Maintain records of fire support and COC activities.
7. Provide guidance on automated information systems relevant to fires.
8. Prepare the fire support plan.
9. Recommend FSCMs to the commander.

REFERENCES:
1. DCOCSOP Digital COC SOP for Battalion Operations in Irregular Warfare
2. MCWP 3-16 Fire Support Coordination in the Ground Combat Element

---

C2OP-COC-2109: Perform as a Communications Watch

EVALUATION-CODED: NO   SUSTAINMENT INTERVAL: 12 months

DESCRIPTION: The communications representative (S6) typically resides in the SYSCON, which is collocated with the COC. They work together with the MAGTF G-6 to ensure the communications architecture will support the unit's operational needs. Single Channel Radio (SCR) nets will vary with each operation. The S-6 will enable connectivity to support resident C2 systems, but is not responsible for maintaining and operating the C2 systems themselves. It is a paramount priority that the S-3, IMO, and S-6 conduct proper planning prior to the operation. The S-6 must continue to communicate with the S-3 and IMO throughout the duration of the operation.

GRADES: SGT, SSGT, GYSGT, 2NDLT, 1STLT, CAPT, MAJ

INITIAL TRAINING SETTING: FORMAL

CONDITION: Given an operational COC, functional communications architecture, current unit TO&E, and C2 systems.

STANDARD: In order to ensure the communications architecture supports the operational requirements.

PERFORMANCE STEPS:
1. Monitor communications architecture.
2. Maintain radio nets.
3. Maintain Switching.
4. Supervise Communication Watch standers.
5. Maintain NIPRnet, SIPRnet and COWAN.
6. Maintain tactical telephone services.
7. Coordinate with Operations Chief/IM Staff to enable C2 systems and collaborative tools.
8. Coordinate outages with technical control facilities. (TECHCONFAC)
9. Develop a communications plan that supports the displacement of the COC.
10. Report communication status.

REFERENCES:
1. DCOCSOP Digital COC SOP for Battalion Operations in Irregular Warfare
2. MCDP 1-0 Marine Corps Operations

C2OP-COC-2110: Perform as a Air Officer

EVALUATION-CODED: NO   SUSTAINMENT INTERVAL: 12 months

DESCRIPTION: The Air O provides coordination between the command and supporting aviation agencies. The Air O works in the FSCC to assist with planning and de-conflicting functions related to air support for the Command. The Air O also advises the commander on aviation capabilities and limitations and prepares requests for air support.

GRADES: CAPT, MAJ

INITIAL TRAINING SETTING: FORMAL

CONDITION: Given an operational COC, functional communications architecture, current unit TO&E, and C2 systems.

STANDARD: To facilitate the six functions of Marine aviation for the supported commander.

PERFORMANCE STEPS:
1. Coordinate between the unit and supporting aviation agencies.
2. Coordinate MEDEVAC/CASEVAC airlift support. (as required)
3. De-conflict fires with other members of the FSCC.
4. Coordinate airlift requirements.
5. Submit JTAR/ASR.
6. Monitor the ATO/ACO.

REFERENCES:
1. DCOCSOP Digital COC SOP for Battalion Operations in Irregular Warfare
2. MCWP 3-2 Aviation Operations

C2OP-LOG-2101: Operate Transportation Capacity Planning Tool (TCPT) as Mission Resource Manager

EVALUATION-CODED: NO   **SUSTAINMENT INTERVAL:** 12 months

DESCRIPTION: Define the term Mission Resource Manager in description. Transportation Capacity Planning Tool (TCPT) allows MAGTF Transportation Planners to view transportation capacity in an online environment through a integrated association of Transportation Movement Request (TMR) and personnel and equipment resources, while providing decision makers with a common operational environment and real-time visibility of resources to enable faster reactions to a dynamic wartime environment.

GRADES: CPL, SGT, SSGT, GYSGT, MSGT, MGYSGT, WO-1, CWO-2, CWO-3, CWO-4, CWO-5, 2NDLT, 1STLT, CAPT, MAJ

INITIAL TRAINING SETTING: FORMAL

CONDITION: Given a functional communications network, a TCPT user account with appropriate permissions and connection to a TCPT server.

STANDARD: To manage movement and lift requirements.

PERFORMANCE STEPS:
1. Manage Personnel Functions.
2. Manage Equipment Functions.
3. Perform Transportation Functions.
4. Perform Mission Tracker Functions.
5. Manage Ground Transportation Requests.

REFERENCES:
1. MCO P4600.7C USMC Transportation Manual
2. TM 11240-15/3F Motor Vehicle Licensing Official's Manual
3. TM 4700-15/1_ Ground Equipment Record Procedures

C2OP-OPER-2101: Operate SharePoint as an Advanced Site Manager

EVALUATION-CODED: NO   **SUSTAINMENT INTERVAL:** 12 months

DESCRIPTION: Advanced SharePoint Site Managers will be able to deliver custom content through graphical dashboards. Advance Site Managers will also optimize Information Management through the use of automation and advanced content manipulation.

GRADES: CPL, SGT, SSGT, GYSGT, 1STSGT, MSGT, MGYSGT, WO-1, CWO-2, CWO-3, CWO-4, CWO-5, 2NDLT, 1STLT, CAPT, MAJ, LTCOL

INITIAL TRAINING SETTING: FORMAL

CONDITION: Given a SharePoint site with appropriate permissions and a functional communications network.

STANDARD: To deliver custom content through graphical dashboards and optimize Information Management through the use of automation and advanced content manipulation.

PERFORMANCE STEPS:
1. Create content types.
2. Manage Slide Library.
3. Configure MySites.
4. Deploy advanced Web Parts.
5. Create Key Performance Indicators (KPIs).
6. Implement advanced calculated columns.
7. Manage Form Library.
8. Implement Workflows.
9. Manage Permissions and Access.

C2OP-OPER-2102: Operate CPoF as an Advanced User

EVALUATION-CODED: NO   **SUSTAINMENT INTERVAL**: 12 months

DESCRIPTION: CPoF is a capability hosted on a computer system that provides collaboration and visualization tools to the COC Staff. CPoF provides situational awareness and aids the commander in decision making, planning, rehearsal, and execution management down to the battalion level.

GRADES: CPL, SGT, SSGT, GYSGT, WO-1, CWO-2, 2NDLT, 1STLT, CAPT

INITIAL TRAINING SETTING: FORMAL

CONDITION: Given an operational CPoF workstation and, a functional CPoF architecture.

STANDARD: To support dissemination of C2 data across the CPoF network.

PERFORMANCE STEPS:
1. Identify the individual component functionality of the CPoF network.
2. Manage received C2 data for dissemination.
3. Employ the features of the CPoF Schedule.
4. Manage shared map presets.
5. Create system reports for dissemination.
6. Employ FTP services.
7. Search the repository.
8. Search the repository database utilizing the CPoF Web Services.
9. Manipulate the Chart features to analyze data.

REFERENCES:
1. CPOF CPoF Installation Guide BC10.0.1
2. CPOF CPoF Web BC10.0.1 Software Version Description (SVD)

3. CPOF DataBridge/C2PC Installation and Administration Guide Version P100 dtd 30 Oct 2009
4. CPOF Installation and Administration Guide for CPOF Data Bridge Version P100 dtd 5 Mar 2010
5. CPOF - Command Sight Users Manual V3.0 Command Sight reference manual
6. CPOF - MAPMAN 3.1.0.0 Administrators Guide Document Ver 1.1
7. CPOF BC10.0.1 CPoF Users Guide Release BC10.0.1
8. CPOF TB-11-7010-409-13 ver 3.0.2 P2 Command Post of the Future (CPOF)
9. CPOF TB-11-7010-464-13 ver QR-1 Command Post of the Future QR-1 (latest version)

C2OP-OPS-2101: Establish the COC

EVALUATION-CODED: NO   **SUSTAINMENT INTERVAL:** 12 months

DESCRIPTION: The Operations Chief is responsible for supervision of setting up the COC and ensuring the COC is fully functioning for the Commander. Typically the Operations Chief will coordinate with G6/S6/IMO for establishing connectivity within the COC and building the network architecture.

GRADES: SSGT, GYSGT, MSGT, MGYSGT

INITIAL TRAINING SETTING: FORMAL

CONDITION: Given the units TO&E, communications architecture, C2 systems, and commander's guidance.

STANDARD: To ensure the COC functions properly to effect Command and Control.

PERFORMANCE STEPS:
1. Identify COC components.
2. Set up COC trailers.
3. Emplace COC tent.
4. Perform trailer maintenance.
5. Perform interior set up of COC equipment.
6. Establish Antenna farm.
7. Establish connectivity.
8. Operate COC visual display equipment.
9. Conduct parallel operation procedures.
10. Troubleshoot common problems.
11. Prepare for Displacement. (as required)

REFERENCES:
1. DCOCSOP Digital COC SOP for Battalion Operations in Irregular Warfare
2. Manufacturer's Technical Instructions and Publications

C2OP-OPS-2102: Establish Identity Dominance with Identity Dominance Systems

EVALUATION-CODED: NO   **SUSTAINMENT INTERVAL:** 6 months

DESCRIPTION: The capability to establish identity dominance in an area of operations requires that the MAGTF commander be able to collect, match, store, and share biometric data. Identity Dominance System satisfies operational requirements as stated by the commander's guidance, current SOPs, and references. BAT provides a means of identifying individuals via fingerprints, iris scan, and photo identification (ID) which enables the creation of individual records. The system includes a laptop with the BAT software, a fingerprint scanner, an iris scanner, a digital camera, and an ID card printer. ID badges can be provided to residents of a city or other identified geographic area. Local residents can be easily identified by friendly forces at entry control points with the use of identification badges. The Marine can access an individual's information such birth date, occupation, place of residence, and any documentation addressing affiliation with anyone involved in terrorist activities. Although BAT may not reside directly in the COC, all COC staff members must be aware of its capabilities.

INITIAL TRAINING SETTING: MOJT

CONDITION: Given current Identity Dominance System with peripherals and associated handheld device(s) and an assigned area of operations.

STANDARD: In order to provide the means to identify persons encountered in a battle space.

PERFORMANCE STEPS:
1. Conduct Maintenance on Dossiers.
2. Conduct enrollments.
3. Conduct Queries.
4. Conduct data mining of information.
5. Maintain a Watchlist (edit/update).
6. Perform preventive maintenance on IDS equipment.
7. Troubleshoot equipment failure.

C2OP-OPS-2103: Prosecute targets via digital means

EVALUATION-CODED: NO   SUSTAINMENT INTERVAL: 12 months

DESCRIPTION:

INITIAL TRAINING SETTING: FORMAL

CONDITION: Given digital fire systems, assets and fire mission

STANDARD: In order to have effects on target.

PERFORMANCE STEPS:
1. Conduct Close Air Support (CAS) Mission.
2. Conduct Artillery fire mission.
3. Conduct Naval Surface Fire Support (NSFS)
4. Conduct HIMARS mission.

C2OP-ATN-2001: Operate the Request for Support (RFS) Application

EVALUATION-CODED: NO   **SUSTAINMENT INTERVAL**: 12 months

DESCRIPTION: The web-based RFS Tracker has two primary functions. Its first function is to enable users to request comprehensive, all-source intelligence analysis products and support from the Counter-IED Operations Integration Center (COIC). RFS Tracker enables the user to submit a detailed request for support, monitor progress, and liaison with the analysts working their request to ensure the end product meets their specific need. Its second function is to enable the user to data-mine historical RFS Tracker products created to satisfy previous users requests.

BILLETS: Commanding Officer, Company Level Intelligence Center Representative, Executive Officer, Information Management Officer, Intelligence Representative, Operations Chief, Operations Officer, Watch Officer/Watch Chief

GRADES: LCPL, CPL, SGT, SSGT, GYSGT, MSGT, MGYSGT, WO-1, CWO-2, CWO-3, CWO-4, CWO-5, 2NDLT, 1STLT

INITIAL TRAINING SETTING: FORMAL

CONDITION: Given a SIPR workstation and access to COIC website.

STANDARD: To mine data and fill intelligence gaps based on Information Requests.

PERFORMANCE STEPS:
1.   Launch the application.
2.   Apply filters for search results.
3.   Retrieve historical RFS DATA.
4.   View a RFS Product.
5.   Submit a new request using the RFS application.

REFERENCES:
1.   MCIP 3-17.02 MAGTF Counter-Improvised Explosive Device Operations
2.   Manufacturer's Technical Instructions and Publications

C2OP-ATN-2002: Operate the Request for Information (RFI) Application

EVALUATION-CODED: NO   **SUSTAINMENT INTERVAL**: 12 months

DESCRIPTION: The Request for Information Application has the capability to request reach-back support by demonstrating the ability to navigate to the COIC-A portal and mine data and fill intelligence gaps. Users can also retrieve and view previously submitted RFS and RFIs.

BILLETS: Commanding Officer, Company Level Intelligence Center Representative, Executive Officer, Intelligence Representative, Operations Chief, Operations Officer, Watch Officer/Watch Chief

GRADES: LCPL, CPL, SGT, SSGT, GYSGT, MSGT, MGYSGT, WO-1, CWO-2, CWO-3, CWO-4, CWO-5, 2NDLT, 1STLT, CAPT

INITIAL TRAINING SETTING: FORMAL

CONDITION: Given a SIPR workstation and access to COIC-A website.

STANDARD: To mine data and fill intelligence gaps based on Information Requests.

PERFORMANCE STEPS:
1. Launch the application.
2. Retrieve historical RFI DATA.
3. Sort a Request for Information (RFI)
4. Submit a new request using the RFI application.

REFERENCES:
1. MCIP 3-17.02 MAGTF Counter-Improvised Explosive Device Operations
2. Manufacturer's Technical Instructions and Publications

C2OP-ATN-2003: Develop a geospatial visualization product

EVALUATION-CODED: NO SUSTAINMENT INTERVAL: 12 months

DESCRIPTION: Google Earth is used as a Geospatial visualization tool and is used to support planning and Information Requirements.

BILLETS: Commanding Officer, Company Level Intelligence Center Representative, Executive Officer, Operations Chief, Operations Officer, Watch Officer/Watch Chief

GRADES: LCPL, CPL, SGT, SSGT, GYSGT, MSGT, MGYSGT, WO-1, CWO-2, CWO-3, CWO-4, CWO-5, 2NDLT, 1STLT, CAPT

INITIAL TRAINING SETTING: FORMAL

CONDITION: Given a SIPR workstation and access to Google Earth.

STANDARD: To support planning and Information Requirements

PERFORMANCE STEPS:
1. Access Google Earth.
2. Apply Google Earth Menu functions.
3. Apply Google Earth Toolbar functions.
4. Apply Illustrate the Search functionality PANES.
5. Apply the Places functionality PANES.
6. Apply the functionality of the Layers PANES.

REFERENCES:
1. Manufacturer's Technical Instructions and Publications

C2OP-ATN-2004: Operate the User Defined Operational Picture (UDOP)
Application

EVALUATION-CODED: NO SUSTAINMENT INTERVAL: 12 months

DESCRIPTION: The User Defined Operational Picture (UDOP) enhances
situational awareness, and allows the user to filter and display data from
multiple tools and links to view a COIC Products.

GRADES: LCPL, CPL, SGT, SSGT, GYSGT, MSGT, MGYSGT, WO-1, CWO-2, CWO-3, CWO-
4, CWO-5, 2NDLT, 1STLT, CAPT, MAJ

INITIAL TRAINING SETTING: FORMAL

CONDITION: Given a SIPR workstation and access to COIC website.

STANDARD: In order to filter and display data to support Information
Requirements.

PERFORMANCE STEPS:
1.   Access the UDOP website.
2.   Access pre-built KMLs.
3.   Navigate through the COCOM, JIEDDO, Community and Quick links folders.
4.   Develop KML through a query.
5.   Display data on a Geospatial tool.

REFERENCES:
1.   MCIP 3-17.02 MAGTF Counter-Improvised Explosive Device Operations
2.   Manufacturer's Technical Instructions and Publications

_____

C2OP-ATN-2005: Operate Web GeoBrowser Application

EVALUATION-CODED: NO SUSTAINMENT INTERVAL: 12 months

DESCRIPTION: Web GeoBrowser is a data mining tool with the ability to
display, correlate, and export shape files for use on geospatial tools.

BILLETS: Commanding Officer, Company Level Intelligence Center
Representative, Executive Officer, Intelligence Representative, Operations
Chief, Operations Officer

GRADES: LCPL, CPL, SGT, SSGT, GYSGT, MSGT, MGYSGT, WO-1, CWO-2, CWO-3, CWO-
4, CWO-5, 2NDLT, 1STLT, CAPT, MAJ

INITIAL TRAINING SETTING: FORMAL

CONDITION: Given a SIPR workstation and access to Web GeoBrowser
application.

STANDARD: In order to data-mine Multi Intelligence Core (MIC) data spatially
and temporarily to support Information Requests.

PERFORMANCE STEPS:
1.   Login to the Web GeoBrowser.
2.   Apply the function of the Web GeoBrowser Menu bar.
3.   Apply the functions of the Web GeoBrowser Tool bar.
4.   Export layers to Shapefiles.

REFERENCES:
1.   MCIP 3-17.02 MAGTF Counter-Improvised Explosive Device Operations
2.   Manufacturer's Technical Instructions and Publications

C2OP-ATN-2006:   Operate 3-D Dashboard application

EVALUATION-CODED: NO   **SUSTAINMENT INTERVAL:**   12 months

DESCRIPTION: 3-D Dashboard is a standalone unclassified application used for viewing and interacting with three-dimensional map models. When combined with operational data the product becomes classified.

GRADES: LCPL, CPL, SGT, SSGT, GYSGT, MSGT, MGYSGT, WO-1, CWO-2, CWO-3, CWO-4, CWO-5, 2NDLT, 1STLT, CAPT, MAJ

INITIAL TRAINING SETTING: FORMAL

CONDITION: Given a SIPR workstation and access to 3D Dashboard application.

STANDARD: To display operational and intelligence data on a three-dimensional model.

PERFORMANCE STEPS:
1.   Launch the 3D Dashboard application.
2.   Load a Map Model from the Main Menu.
3.   Navigate 3d Map Model.
4.   Import data.
5.   Apply graphic tools.
6.   Display final product.

REFERENCES:
1.   MCIP 3-17.02 MAGTF Counter-Improvised Explosive Device Operations
2.   Manufacturer's Technical Instructions and Publications

C2OP-ATN-2007:   Operate Cell Pack Application

EVALUATION-CODED: NO   **SUSTAINMENT INTERVAL:**   12 months

DESCRIPTION: Cell Pack application is used to data mine CELEX database, provide first order association and display the results in a HTML format. First Order Association is defined as a relationship between related phone numbers.

INITIAL TRAINING SETTING: FORMAL

CONDITION: Given a SIPR workstation and access to the Cell Pack application.

STANDARD: To identify telephonic first order associations.

PERFORMANCE STEPS:
1.   Launch application.
2.   Apply SEARCH PARAMETERS.
3.   Review a report.
4.   Analyze reported data.

REFERENCES:
1.   Manufacturer's Technical Instructions and Publications

C2OP-ATN-2008:   Operate Global Name Recognition (GNR) Application

EVALUATION-CODED: NO   **SUSTAINMENT INTERVAL**: 12 months

DESCRIPTION: Global Name Recognition application allows the user to complete a name search within multiple databases, perform name analysis, and identify name variances.

GRADES: LCPL, CPL, SGT, SSGT, GYSGT, MSGT, MGYSGT, WO-1, CWO-2, CWO-3, CWO-4, CWO-5, 2NDLT, 1STLT, CAPT, MAJ

INITIAL TRAINING SETTING: FORMAL

CONDITION: Given a SIPR workstation and access to Global Name Recognition application.

STANDARD: In order to gather information related to a named person of interest (NPIs).

PERFORMANCE STEPS:
1.   Launch Global Name Recognition application.
2.   Establish Search parameters.
3.   Generate a report related to a named person of interest (NPIs)

REFERENCES:
1.   MCIP 3-17.02 MAGTF Counter-Improvised Explosive Device Operations
2.   Manufacturer's Technical Instructions and Publications

C2 T&R MANUAL

APPENDIX A

ACRONYMS AND ABBREVIATIONS

ABP . . . . Air Battle Plan
AFATDS . . . . Advanced Field Artillery Tactical Data System
AO . . . . Area of Operation
AO/AOR . . . . Area of Operation/Area of Responsibility
AODB . . . . Air Operations Database
AOI . . . . .Area of Interest
AOR . . . . .Area of Responsibility
ASL . . . . .Air Support List
ASOC . . . . Air Support Operations Center
BAT . . . . Biometric Automated Toolset
BCS3 . . . . Battle Command Support Sustainment System
BFT . . . . Blue Force Tracking
C2 . . . . Command and Control
C2PC . . . . Command and Control Personal Computer
CBAE . . . . commander's battlespace area evaluation
CCIR . . . . .Commander's Critical Information Requirement
CIS . . . . .Combat Intelligence System
CLC2S . . . . Common Logistics Command and Control System
CO . . . . Commanding Officer
COA . . . . .Course of Action
COC . . . . .Combat Operations Center
CP . . . . .Command Post
CPoF . . . . .Command Post of the Future
CTAPS . . . . Contingency Theater Automated Planning System
CTP . . . . Common Tactical Picture
DCOCSOP . . . . Digital COC SOP
DoD . . . . Department of Defense
DoDI . . . . Department Of Defense Instruction
DoN . . . . .Department Of the Navy
DRRS . . . . .Defense Readiness Reporting System
DSTB . . . . .Decision Support Toolbox
EDL . . . . .Equipment Density List
EEFI . . . . .Essential Elements of Friendly Information
EMMCP . . . . .Execution Management Map Control Panel
EMT . . . . Effects Management Tool
ESTAT . . . . Execution Status and Monitoring Application
FDC . . . . fire direction center
FDP&E . . . . Force Deployment Planning & Execution
FM . . . . Army Field Manual
FMFM . . . . .Fleet Marine Force Manual
FRAGO . . . . Fragmentary Order
FSTAT . . . . Force Status and Monitoring Application
GCCGS . . . . Global Command and Control System
GNR . . . . Global Name Recognition
HAS . . . . Higher, Adjacent, Subordinate
HTML . . . . .Hyper Text Markup Language
IERS . . . . information exchange requirements
IM . . . . .Information Management

```
IMP . . . . . . . . . . . . . . . . . . . . . . . . . . . . Information Management Planning
INST . . . . . . . . . . . . . . . . . . . . . . . . . . . . . . . . . . . . . . . . Install
IO . . . . . . . . . . . . . . . . . . . . . . . . . . . . . . . . . Information Operation
IOSV1 . . . . . . . . . . . . . . . . . . . . .Intelligence Operations Server Version 1
IOT . . . . . . . . . . . . . . . . . . . . . . . . . . . . . . . . . . . . . In order to
IR . . . . . . . . . . . . . . . . . . . . . . . . . . . . . . . . intelligence requirements
ITV . . . . . . . . . . . . . . . . . . . . . . . . . . . . . . . . . in-transit visibility
JADOCS . . . . . . . . . Joint Automated Deep Operations Coordination System
JBV . . . . . . . . . . . . . . . . . . . . . . . . . . . . Joint Battle Space Viewer
JIIM . . . . . . . . .Joint, Interagency, Intergovernmental, Multinational
JTCW . . . . . . . . . . . . . . Joint Tactical Common Operation Workstation
KPI . . . . . . . . . . . . . . . . . . . . . . . . . . . .Key Performance Indicators
MAGTF . . . . . . . . . . . . . . . . . . . . . . . . . .Marine Air-Ground Task Force
MAIN . . . . . . . . . . . . . . . . . . . . . . . . . . . . . . . . . . . . . .Maintain
MCDP . . . . . . . . . . . . . . . . . . . . . . . .Marine Corps Doctrinal Publication
MCIP . . . . . . . . . . . . . . . . . . . . . . . .Marine Corps Information Publication
MCO . . . . . . . . . . . . . . . . . . . . . . . . . . . . .Marine Corps Order
MCPP . . . . . . . . . . . . . . . . . . . . . . . . . Marine Corps Planning Process
MCRP . . . . . . . . . . . . . . . . . . . . . . . .Marine Corps Reference Publication
MCWP . . . . . . . . . . . . . . . . . . . . . . . .Marine Corps Warfighting Publication
MET . . . . . . . . . . . . . . . . . . . . . . . . . . . .Mission Essential Task
METL . . . . . . . . . . . . . . . . . . . . . . . . . Mission Essential Task List
METT-T . . . . . . . . . .Mission, Enemy, Terrain, Troops & Time Available
MISTC . . . . . . . . . . . . . . . . .MAGTF Integrated Systems Training Center
MOE . . . . . . . . . . . . . . . . . . . . . . . . . . . .Measure Of Effectiveness
MOJT . . . . . . . . . . . . . . . . . . . . . . . . . . .Manage On the Job Training
MOP . . . . . . . . . . . . . . . . . . . . . . . . . . . .Measure Of Performance
NAVMC . . . . . . . . . . . . . . . . . . . . . . . . . . . . Navy Marine Corps
NPI . . . . . . . . . . . . . . . . . . . . . . . . . . . .named person of interest
NSFS . . . . . . . . . . . . . . . . . . . . . . . . . .Naval Surface Fire Support
OPER . . . . . . . . . . . . . . . . . . . . . . . . . . . . . . . . . . Operate
OPORD . . . . . . . . . . . . . . . . . . . . . . . . . . . .Operations Order
OPS . . . . . . . . . . . . . . . . . . . . . . . . . . . . . . . . . .Operations
OPT . . . . . . . . . . . . . . . . . . . . . . . . . . Operational Planning Team
ORM . . . . . . . . . . . . . . . . . . . . . . . . . . Operational Risk management
OS . . . . . . . . . . . . . . . . . . . . . . . . . . . . . . .Operating System
PAE . . . . . . . . . . . . . . . . . . . . . . . . . Plans Application Extension
PCC . . . . . . . . . . . . . . . . . . . . . . . . . . . . pre-combat checks
PCI . . . . . . . . . . . . . . . . . . . . . . . . . . . .pre-combat inspections
PLAN . . . . . . . . . . . . . . . . . . . . . . . . . . . . . . . . . .Planning
R2P2 . . . . . . . . . . . . . . . . . . . . . . . . . Rapid Response Planning Process
RFI . . . . . . . . . . . . . . . . . . . . . . . . . . . . request for information
RFS . . . . . . . . . . . . . . . . . . . . . . . . . . . . . request for support
RRTS+ . . . . . . . . . . . . . . . . . . . . . . . . Rapid Request Tracking System
RSO&I . . . . . . . . .Reception, Staging, Onward Movement, and Integration
SAT . . . . . . . . . . . . . . . . . . . . . . . . . . . .Systems Approach to Training
SCL . . . . . . . . . . . . . . . . . . . . . . . . . . Standard Configuration Load
SIPR . . . . . . . . . . . . . . . . . . . . . . . . . Secure Internet Protocol Router
SOP . . . . . . . . . . . . . . . . . . . . . . . . . . .Standard Operating Procedure
SYSADMIN . . . . . . . . . . . . . . . . . . . . . . . . . System administration
T&R . . . . . . . . . . . . . . . . . . . . . . . . . . .Training and Readiness
TACP . . . . . . . . . . . . . . . . . . . . . . . . . . .Tactical Air Control Party
TBMCS . . . . . . . . . . . . . . . . . . . . Theater Battle Management Core System
TCPT . . . . . . . . . . . . . . . . . . . . . Transportation Capacity Planning Tool
TM . . . . . . . . . . . . . . . . . . . . . . . . . . . . . . .Technical Manual
```

TMR . . . . Transportation Movement Request
TOECR . . . . .Table of Organization and Equipment Change Request
TO/E . . . . Table of Organization/Equipment
TPFDD . . . . Time-Phased Force Deployment Data
UCP . . . . Universal Communication Processor
UDOP . . . . .User Defined Operational Picture
UNTL . . . . Universal Naval Task List
UTM . . . . .Unit Training Management
UTO . . . . .Unit Task Organization
WAG . . . . , ...Wide Area Geographic
WARP . . . . Web Air Request Processor
WO . . . . Watch Officer
WC . . . . Watch Chief

C2 T&R MANUAL

APPENDIX B
.
TERMS AND DEFINITIONS

Terms in this glossary are subject to change as applicable orders and directives are revised. Terms established by Marine Corps orders or directives take precedence after definitions found in Joint Pub 1-02, DOD Dictionary of Military and Associated Terms.

A

After Action Review (AAR). A professional discussion of training events conducted after all training to promote learning among training participants. The formality and scope increase with the command level and size of the training evolution. For longer exercises, they should be planned for at predetermined times during an exercise. The results of the AAR shall be recorded on an after action report and forwarded to higher headquarters. The commander and higher headquarters use the results of an AAR to reallocate resources, reprioritize their training plan, and plan for future training.

C

Chaining. A process that enables unit leaders to effectively identify subordinate collective events and individual events that support a specific collective event. For example, collective training events at the 4000-level are directly supported by collective events at the 3000-level. Utilizing the building block approach to progressive training, these collective events are further supported by individual training events at the 1000 and 2000-levels. When a higher-level event by its nature requires the completion of lower level events, they are "chained"; Sustainment credit is given for all lower level events chained to a higher event.

D

Deception. Those measures designed to mislead the enemy by manipulation, distortion, or falsification of evidence to induce the enemy to react in a manner prejudicial to the enemy's interests. (JP 1-02)

E

E-Coded Event. An "E-Coded" event is a collective T&R event that is a noted indicator of capability or, a noted Collective skill that contributes to the unit's ability to perform the supported MET. As such, only "E-Coded" events are assigned a CRP value and used to calculate a unit's CRP.

I

Individual Readiness. The individual training readiness of each Marine is measured by the number of individual events required and completed for the rank or billet currently held.

M

Marine Corps Combat Readiness and Evaluation System (MCCRES). An evaluation system designed to provide commanders with a comprehensive set of mission performance standards from which training programs can be developed; and through which the efficiency and effectiveness of training can be evaluated. The Ground T&R Program will eventually replace MCCRES.

O

Operational Readiness (OR). (DoD or NATO) OR is the capability of a unit/formation, ship, weapon system, or equipment to perform the missions or functions for which it is organized or designed. May be used in a general sense or to express a level or degree of readiness.

P

Performance Step. Performance steps are included in the components of an Individual T&R Event. They are the major procedures (i.e., actions) a Marine unit must accomplish to perform an individual event to standard. They describe the procedure the task performer must take to perform the task under operational conditions and provide sufficient information for a task performer to perform the procedure (may necessitate identification of supporting steps, procedures, or actions in outline form). Performance steps follow a logical progression and should be followed sequentially, unless otherwise stated. Normally, performance steps are listed only for 1000-level individual events (those that are taught in the entry-level MOS school). Listing performance steps is optional if the steps are already specified in a published reference.

R

Readiness. (DoD) Readiness is the ability of U.S. military forces to fight and meet the demands of the national military strategy. Readiness is the synthesis of two distinct but interrelated levels: (a) Unit readiness--The ability to provide capabilities required by combatant commanders to execute assigned missions. This is derived from the ability of each unit to deliver the outputs for which it was designed. (b) Joint readiness--The combatant commander's ability to integrate and synchronize ready combat and support forces to execute assigned missions.

S

Section Skill Tasks. Section skills are those competencies directly related to unit functioning. They are group rather than individual in nature, and require participation by a section (S-1, S-2, S-3, etc).

T

Training Task. This describes a direct training activity that pertains to an individual Marine. A task is composed of 3 major components: a description of what is to be done, a condition, and a standard.

U

Unit CRP. Unit CRP is a percentage of the E-coded collective events that support the unit METL accomplished by the unit. Unit CRP is the average of all MET CRP.

W

Waived Event. An event that is waived by a commanding officer when in his or her judgment, previous experience or related performance satisfies the requirement of a particular event.

APPENDIX C

REFERENCES

Marine Corps Doctrinal Publication (MCDP)
MCDP 5 Planning
MCDP 6 Command and Control

Marine Corps Requirement Publications (MCRP)

Marine Corps Warfighting Publications (MCWPs)
MCWP 1-0 Marine Corps Operation
MCWP 2-1 Intelligence Operation
MCWP 3-1 Ground Combat Operation
MCWP 3-2 Aviation Operations
MCWP 3-16 Fire Support Coordination in the Ground Combat Element
MCWP 4-1 Logistics Operation
MCWP 5-1 Marine Corps Planning Process
MCWP 6-2 MAGTF Command and Control Operation

Marine Corps Order (MCO)
MCO 3500.26A Universal Naval Task List (UNTL) Version 3.0 (Jan 07)
MCO 3500.27_ Operational Risk Management (ORM)
MCO 4105.4 Ground Weapon Systems/Equipment (WS/E) and Automated Information
    Systems (AIS) Life Cycle Logistics Support
MCO P4400.150_ Consumer Level Supply Policy Manual
MCO P4600.7C USMC Transportation Manual
MCO P4790.2_ MIMMS Field Procedures Manual

Marine Corps Information Publication (MCIP)
MCIP 3-17.02 MAGTF Counter-Improvised Explosive Device Operations

Fleet Marine Force Manual (FMFM)
FMFM 4-1 Combat Service Support Operations (PCN 13900027300)

Technical Manual (TM)
TM 11-7025-279-10-1 AFATDS Users Manual
TM 4700-15/1_ Ground Equipment Record Procedures
TM 11180A-OI/4 TECHNICAL MANUAL/OPERATOR AND FIELD MAINTENANCE MANUAL
    INCLUDING REPAIR PARTS AND SPECIAL TOOLS LIST FORFORCE XXI BATTLE COMMAND
    BRIGADE-AND-BELOW (FBCB2)-BLUEFORCE TRACKING (BFT) TACTICAL OPERATIONS
    CENTER (TOC) SYSTEM
TM 11180A-OR TECHNICAL MANUAL/OPERATORS MANUAL FORFORCE XXI BATTLE COMMAND
    BRIGADE-AND-BELOW(FBCB2)-BLUE FORCE TRACKING COMPUTER SET, DIGITALAN/UYK-
    128(V) AN/UYK-128(V)1(NSN: 7010-01-475-5277) (EIC:K2S)AN/UYK-128(V)3
    (NSN: 7010-01-513-8459) (EIC:K2U) DISTRIBUTION
TM I1180A-OR   Technical Manual Operator's Manual for Force XXI Battle
    Command Brigade-and-Below (FBCB2)-Blue Force Tracking (BFT) Computer Set,
    Digital AN/UYK-128(V) AN/UYK-128(V)1 (NSN: 7010-01-475-5277) (EIC:K2S)
    AN/UYK-128(V)3 (NSN: 7010-01-513-8459) (EIC:K2U)
TM 11240-15/3F Motor Vehicle Licensing Official's Manual

Miscellaneous

BAT IAW Biometric Automated Tool Set User Guide
Battle Command and Sustainment Support System (BCS3)
      https://logmod.hqmc.usmc.mil/bridge/bcs3.html
CPOF - Command Sight Users Manual V3.0 Command Sight reference manual
CPOF - MAPMAN 3.1.0.0 Administrators Guide Document Ver 1.1
CPOF TB-11-7010-409-13 ver 3.0.2 P2 Command Post of the Future (CPOF)
CPOF TB-11-7010-464-13 ver QR-1 Command Post of the Future QR-1 (latest
      version)
DCOCSOP Digital COC SOP for Battalion Operations in Irregular Warfare
JADOCS ver 1.0.3.5 Build 25 Mar 2008 Joint Automated Deep Operations
      Coordination System
Manufacturer's Operating Instructions
Manufacturer's Technical Instructions and Publications
MEF C2 Systems Integration Plan Marine Expeditionary Force Command and
      Control Systems Integration Plan Mar 2006
TB 11-7025-297-10 AFATDS Operators Notebook
TB 11-7010-326-10 BFT FBCB2 Operator's Pocket Guide (Draft) 17 February 2004
TB 11-7010-326-10-3 TECHNICAL BULLETIN FBCB2/BFT OPERATOR'S POCKET GUIDE
      FORForce XXI Battle Command Brigade-and-Below Blue Force Tracking
      (FBCB2/BFT) Computer Set, Digital AN/UYK-128(V)

C2 T&R MANUAL

APPENDIX D

TRAINING BY BILLET IN THE REGT/BN COC

C2 Training Requirements by Billet in the Regt/Bn COC

Billet	EQC		COC Equipment Operations			TCOT				Leader's Courses				Sys Admin		Battle Staff Training
	C2PC BFT Tools	AFATDS	CPOF	BFT CLC2S	BCS3 Level I & II	TBMCS	JADOCS	ENT & II	Share Point Level I WK	Commanders C2 Systems Overview	IWO CPOF	Share Point Level III	BFT UNI IOS v1	AFCOCS	
CO	2	2							2	1					3
XO	2	2					2	2	2	1					3
S3	2	2	2				2	2	2	1	2				3
Ops Chief	2	2	1				2	2	2	2	2				3
Watch Officer	2		2					2	2	1	2				3
Watch Chief	2		2	2	2		2	2	2	1	2				3
S3 Journal Clerk	1		1	1	2		2	2	2		2				3
CTP/CPOF Operator	1	1	1	1				2	2		2	2			3
FSC	1	2	2			1	2	2	2	2	2	2		2	3
AirO	2	2	2				2	2	2		2	2		2	3
Adj LNO	2	2	2			2	2	2	2		2	2		2	3
Its Rep	2	2	2				2	2	2						3
Fires Clerk	2	1	2				2	2	2				2		3
WebO	2		2				2	2	2	2	2		2	2	3
ASST Representatives	2	2		2		1	1	2	2	2	2				3
Naval Officer															
Radio Operator	1		2						2			2			3
S2 Representative	2	1	2	2			2	2	2	2		2			3
S1 Representative	2	2	2		2				2	2				2	3
S4 Representative	2	2	2	1	1				2	2				1	3
S6 Officer	2	2	2	2					2	2					3

1: REQUIRED

2: RECOMMENDED

3: REQUIRED AS A COLLECTIVE TRAINING EVENT FOR THE STAFF FOLLOWING INITIAL INDIVIDUAL TRAINING

Jan 2011